TATTING
DOILIES & EDGINGS

edited by
Rita Weiss

Dover Publications, Inc.
New York

Published in Canada by General Publishing Company, Ltd.,
30 Lesmill Road, Don Mills, Toronto, Ontario.
Published in the United Kingdom by Constable and Company, Ltd., 10 Orange Street, London WC2H 7EG.

This Dover edition, first published in 1980, is a new selection
of patterns from *The Tatting Book. Book 111*, published by the
Spool Cotton Company, 1938; *Tatted & Crocheted Designs*,
published by the American Thread Company, 1944; *Tatting*,
published by the Spool Cotton Company, 1939; *Doilies,
Crocheted and Tatted. Star Book No. 44*, published by the
American Thread Company (n.d.); *Star Gift Book. No. 31*, published by the American Thread Company, 1944; *Chair Backs.
Star Book No. 46*, published by the American Thread Company (n.d.); *Star Needlework Journal, Vol. 5, No. 4*, published
by the American Thread Company, 1920.

International Standard Book Number: 0-486-24051-7
Library of Congress Catalog Card Number: 80-66611

Manufactured in the United States of America
Dover Publications, Inc.
180 Varick Street
New York, N.Y. 10014

INTRODUCTION

There is nothing quite so elegant as a piece of delicate tatting. From lovely edgings or an occasional doily to a chair set or luncheon mats, this heirloom lace adds grace to your accessories or to your home. Even though a tatted article looks fragile and lace-like, it will be exceedingly strong and capable of withstanding much rough use. Unlike crocheting and knitting where each stitch is somewhat dependent upon its neighbor, and one becoming unfastened endangers the rest of the stitches, the stitches of tatting are isolated, and are very difficult to undo when once formed.

This is a new collection of some of the most lovely tatted doily and edging patterns published in instruction brochures over thirty years ago, during a period when the making of all types of lace was an extremely popular pastime. Today, as we return once again to the joys of creating exquisite handmade articles, tatting is once again enjoying a new surge of popularity.

Tatting consists of so few different stitches that it is extremely simple; and it requires very little concentration once the stitches have been mastered. It is actually composed only of knots—or stitches—and loops—or picots—which are drawn up into circles or semi-circles. Varied arrangements of these figures produce different kinds of patterns. If you have never tatted before, or if you need a refresher course, complete instructions on how to tat appear on pages 46 and 47. Tatting also has the great advantage of being very portable; it can be worked on for a few minutes and then put down again without becoming disarranged—an impossibility with most types of lacemaking.

First introduced over 200 years ago, tatting was an attempt to reproduce the knotted laces of the sixteenth century. In knotted lace, the work is made over a cord with the cotton forming it wound upon a netting needle; in tatting, however, the stitches are made over a thread, and the thread is wound upon a shuttle small enough to allow its being passed easily backwards and forwards over and under the thread upon which the stitches are being formed. The origin of the English word "tatting" is rather obscure. Possibly it is taken from the word "tatters" denoting the fragile, disjointed nature of the little motifs made separately and then joined together into patterns. In most of Europe, tatting is called "frivolité"; the Italians, however, call it by a more descriptive word, "occhi" (eyes). In the Far East, the craft still retains the ancient designation of "makouk" from the shuttles upon which it is executed.

Since the patterns in this book all come from old instruction brochures, many of the threads listed with the patterns may no longer be available. Other threads of similar weight may be substituted. Check with your local needlework shop or department. Whatever type of thread you decide to use, be certain to buy at one time sufficient thread of the same dye lot to complete the project you wish to make. It is often impossible to match shades later as dye lots vary.

When you have completed your project, it should be washed and blocked. No matter how carefully you have worked, blocking will give your tatting a more "professional" look. Use a good neutral soap or detergent and make suds in cool water. Wash by squeezing the suds through the project, but do not rub. Rinse two or three times in clear water, if desired. Starching the project will give it a crisper look. Using rustproof pins, pin the article right side down on a well-padded surface. Be sure to pin out all picots, loops, scallops, etc. When the project is almost completely dry, press through a damp cloth with a moderately hot iron. Do not rest the iron on the decorative, raised stitches! When thoroughly dry, remove the pins.

RUFFLED DOILY

Make this doily with any of the AMERICAN THREAD COMPANY products listed below:

Material	Quantity	Approx. Size of Doily without Ruffle
"STAR" TATTING CROCHET Article 25 or	3 balls White	5½ inches in diameter
"STAR" CROCHET COTTON Article 20, Size 30 or	1 ball White	8 inches in diameter
"GEM" CROCHET COTTON Article 35, Size 30	1 ball White	8 inches in diameter
1 Shuttle		

Center: R, 1 d, 8 p sep by 2 ds, 1 d, cl r, tie and cut.

1st Round—R, 2 ds, p, 2 ds, join to any p of center, 2 ds, p, 2 ds, cl r, * turn. Ch, 5 ds, 3 p sep by 3 ds, 5 ds, turn. R, 2 ds, join to last p of last r, 2 ds, join to next p of center, 2 ds, p, 2 ds, cl r, repeat from * all around joining last p of last r to 1st p of 1st r, tie and cut.

2nd Round—R, 3 ds, 3 p sep by 2 ds, 3 ds, p, 3ds, 3 p sep by 2 ds, 3 ds, cl r, * turn. Ch, 5 ds, 3 p sep by 3 ds, 5 ds, turn. R, 3 ds, p, 2 ds, join to next to last p of last r, 2 ds, p, 3 ds, join to middle p of ch of 1st round, 3 ds, 3 p sep by 2 ds, 3 ds, cl r, turn. Ch, 5 ds, 3 p sep by 3 ds, 5 ds, turn. R, 3 ds, p, 2 ds, join to next to last p of last r, 2 ds, p, 3 ds, p, 3 ds, 3 p sep by 2 ds, 3 ds, cl r. Repeat from * all around having 16 rings in round and joining every other r to middle p of ch of 1st round, tie and cut.

3rd Round—* R, 2 ds, 3 p sep by 2 ds, 2 ds, join to middle p of ch of previous round, 2 ds, 3 p sep by 2 ds, 2 ds, cl r, turn. Ch, 5 ds, 5 p sep by 3 ds, 5 ds, turn. Repeat from * all around, tie and cut.

4th Round—* R, 2 ds, 3 p sep by 2 ds, 2 ds, join to middle p of ch of last round, 2 ds, 3 p sep by 2 ds, 2 ds, cl r, turn. Ch, 5 ds, 7 p sep by 3 ds, 5 ds, turn. Repeat from * all around, tie and cut.

5th Round—* R, 4 ds, p, 4 ds, join to 6th p of ch of last round, 4 ds, p, 4 ds, cl r, turn. Ch, 5 ds, 3 p sep by 3 ds, 5 ds, turn. R, 4 ds, p, 4 ds, join to 2nd p of same ch of last round, 4 ds, p, 4 ds, cl r, turn. Ch, 5 ds, 3 p sep by 3 ds, 5 ds, turn. Repeat from * all around, tie and cut.

6th Round—Same as 3rd round.

7th Round—**Start Ruffle:** * R, 7 ds, join to 5th p of ch of last round, 7 ds, cl r, turn. Ch, 5 ds, 5 p sep by 3 ds, 5 ds, turn. R, 7 ds, join to center p of same ch, 7 ds, cl r, turn. Ch, 5 ds, 5 p sep by 3 ds, 5 ds, turn. R, 7 ds, join to 1st p of same ch, 7 ds, cl r, turn. Ch, 5 ds, 5 p sep by 3 ds, 5 ds, turn. Repeat from * all around, tie and cut.

8th Round—* R, 2 ds, p, 2 ds, join to 4th p of ch of last round, 2 ds, p, 2 ds, cl r, turn. Ch, 3 ds, 5 p sep by 2 ds, 3 ds, turn. R, 2 ds, p, 2 ds, join to 2nd p of same ch, 2 ds, p, 2 ds, cl r, turn. Ch, 3 ds, 5 p sep by 2 ds, 3 ds, turn. Repeat from * all around, tie and cut.

9th Round—Same as last round.

DIRECTIONS FOR STARCHING DOILIES

Starch: Dissolve ¼ cup starch in ½ cup of cold water. Boil about 1¼ cups of water, remove from flame, then slowly stir the starch mixture into boiling water stirring constantly. Place back on flame until it thickens.

As soon as starch is cool enough to handle, dip doily and squeeze starch through it thoroughly. Wring out extra starch. The doily should be wet with starch but there should be none in the spaces. Pin center of doily in position according to size and leave until thoroughly dry. If steam iron is used iron ruffle after it is dry. If regular iron is used dampen ruffle slightly before pressing. Pin folds of ruffle in position and leave until thoroughly dry.

LACY DOILIES

Round Tatted Doily

Materials Required — AMERICAN THREAD COMPANY "STAR" MERCERIZED CROCHET COTTON, Article 30, Size 50.

2—150 yd. Balls White.

1 Shuttle and Ball.

Doily measures about 8½ inches.

R, 1 d, 12 p sep by 1 d, 1 d, cl r, cut and tie.

1st Row. R, 4 d, join to p of small r, 4 d, cl r. Ch, 6 d, turn. R, 6 d, 5 p sep by 2 d, 6 d, cl r, turn. * Ch, 6 d, turn. R, 4 d, join to next p of small r, 4 d, cl r, turn. Ch, 6 d, turn. R, 6 d, join to last p of last large r made, 2 d, 4 p sep by 2 d, 6 d, cl r, turn. Repeat from * all around joining last large r to 1st large r made, turn. Ch, 6 d, cut and tie.

2nd Row. R, 4 d, join to 3rd p of large r of 1st row, 4 d, cl r. Ch, 6 d, turn. R, 2 d, 7 p sep by 2 d, 2 d, cl r. * R, 2 d, join to last p of last r made, 2 d, 6 p sep by 2 d, 2 d, cl r. R, 2 d join to last p of last r made, 2 d, 6 p sep by 2 d, 2 d, cl r, (clover) turn. Ch, 6 d, turn. R, 4 d, join to 1st p of next large r of 1st row, 4 d, cl r, turn. Ch, 6 d, turn. R, 4 d, skip 1 p, join to next p of same r, 4 d, cl r, turn. Ch, 6 d, turn. R, 2 d, 3 p sep by 2 d, 2 d, join to center p of 3rd r of clover, 2 d, 3 p sep by 2 d, 2 d, cl r. Repeat from * 10 times. R, 2 d, join to last p of last r made, 2 d, 6 p sep by 2 d, 2 d, cl r. R, 2 d, join to last p of last r made, 2 d, 6 p sep by 2 d, 2 d, join to center p of 1st r made, 2 d, 3 p sep by 2 d, 2 d, cl r, turn. Ch, 6 d, turn. R, 4 d, join to 1st p of next r, 4 d, cl r, turn. Ch, 6 d, cut and tie.

3rd Row. R, 5 d, p, 5 d, join to center p of center r of clover, 5 d, p, 5 d, cl r, turn. ** Ch, 8 d, p, 8 d, turn. * R, 5 d, join to last p of last r made, 5 d, 2 p sep by 5 d, 5 d, cl r, turn. Ch, 8 d, p, 8 d, turn. R, 5 d, join to last p of last r made, 5 d, join to center p of next clover, 5 d, p, 5 d, cl r and repeat from ** in same manner all around, cut and tie.

4th Row. R, 3 d, p, 3 d, join to p of ch of 3rd row, 3 d, p, 3 d, cl r. Ch, 6 d, turn. * R, 3 d, 3 p sep by 3 d, 3 d, cl r, turn. Ch, 6 d. R, 3 d, p, 3 d, join to p of next ch of 3rd row, 3 d, p, 3 d, cl r. Ch, 6 d, p, 6 d, p, 6 d, turn. R, 3 d, 3 p sep by 3 d, 3 d, cl r. R, 3 d, join to last p of last r made, 3 d, 4 p sep by 3 d, 3 d, cl r. R, 3 d, join to last p of last r made, 3 d, p, 3 d, p, 3 d, cl r, turn. Ch, 6 d, join to corresponding p of opposite ch, 6 d, p, 6 d. R, 3 d, p, 3 d, join to p of next ch of 3rd row, 3 d, p, 3 d cl r. Ch, 6 d, turn. Repeat from * all around in same manner, cut and tie.

5th Row. R, 6 d, 3 p sep by 6 d, 6 d, cl r, turn. * Ch, 6 d, 5 p sep by 3 d, 6 d. R, 6 d, p, 6 d, cl r, turn. Ch, 6 d, 2 p sep by 3 d, 3 d, join to 3rd p of previous r made, 3 d, 2 p sep by 3 d, 6 d, turn. R, 3 d, 5 p sep by 3 d, 3 d, cl r. R, 3 d, join to last p of last r made, 3 d, 4 p sep by 3 d, 3 d, cl r, turn. Ch, 6 d, 6 p sep by 3 d, 3 d. R, 3 d, join to last p of ch just made, 3 d, p, 3 d, join to 2nd p

of 3rd r of clover of 4th row, 3 d, 2 p sep by 3 d, 3 d, cl r. R, 3 d, join to last p of last r made, 3 d, p, 3 d, join to center p of small r between clovers of 4th row, 3 d, 2 p sep by 3 d, 3 d, cl r. R, 3 d, join to last p of last r made, 3 d, p, 3 d, join to center p of 1st r of next clover, 3 d, 2 p sep by 3 d, 3 d, cl r. Ch, 3 d, join to last p of last r made, 3 d, 5 p sep by 3 d, 6 d, turn. R, 3 d, 2 p sep by 3 d, 3 d, join to the 3rd free p of corresponding r, 3 d, join to next p of same r, 3 d, p, 3 d, cl r. R, 3 d, join to last p of last r made, 3 d, join to next free p of next r, 3 d, join to next p of same r, 3 d, 2 p sep by 3 d, 3 d, cl r, turn. Ch, 6 d, 5 p sep by 3 d, 6 d, turn. R, 6 d, join to p of corresponding r, 6 d, cl r, turn. Ch, 6 d, 5 p sep by 3 d, 6 d, turn. R, 6 d, join to center free p of 2nd last ch made, 6 d, p, 6 d, p, 6 d, cl r, turn. Repeat from * all around in same manner, cut and tie.

6th Row. R, 6 d, join in p between two small rings, 6 d, cl r, * turn. Ch, 6 d, 5 p sep by 3 d, 6 d, join in center p of ch of 5th row, 6 d, 5 p sep by 3 d, 6 d, join to center p of next ch, 6 d, 5 p sep by 3 d, 6 d, turn. R, 6 d, join in p between two small rings, 6 d, cl r. Repeat from * all around in same manner, cut and tie.

Oval Tatted Doily

Materials Required — AMERICAN THREAD COMPANY "STAR" MERCERIZED CROCHET COTTON, Article 30, Size 50.

2—150 yd. Balls White or Ecru.

1 Shuttle and 1 Ball.

Doily measures about 11¼ x 8½ inches.

R, 4 d, 5 p sep by 2 d, 4 d, cl r, turn. Ch, 6 d, turn. R, 3 d, 3 p sep by 2 d, 3 d, cl r, turn. * Ch, 6 d, turn. R, 4 d, join to last p of large r, 2 d, 4 p sep by 2 d, 4 d, cl r, turn. Ch, 6 d, turn. R, 3 d, join to 3rd p of small r, 2 d, 2 p sep by 2 d, 3 d, cl r, turn. Repeat from * 11 times. Ch, 6 d, turn. * R, 4 d, join to last p of last large r, 2 d, 4 p sep by 2 d, 4 d, cl r. Repeat from *. Ch, 6 d, join to next free p of small r, 6 d, turn. * R, 4 d, join to last p of large r, 2 d, 4 p sep by 2 d, 4 d, cl r. Repeat from * twice, turn. Ch, 6 d, join to same p of same small r, 6 d, turn. * R, 4 d, join to last p of large r, 2 d, 4 p sep by 2 d, 4 d, cl r. Repeat from *. Ch, 6 d, join to next free p of same small r, 6 d, turn. * R, 4 d, join to last p of large r, 2 d, 4 p sep by 2 d, 4 d, cl r. Ch, 6 d, join to free p of next small r, 6 d, turn. Repeat from * 11 times. * R, 4 d, join to last p of large r, 2 d, 4 p sep by 2 d, 4 d, cl r. Repeat from *. Ch, 6 d, join to next free p of same r, 6 d. * R, 4 d, join to last p of large r, 2 d, 4 p sep by 2 d, 4 d, cl r. Repeat from * twice. Ch, 6 d, join to same p of small r, 6 d, turn. R, 4 d, join to last p of large r, 2 d, 3 p sep by 2 d, join to corresponding p of 1st large r, 4 d, cl r, cut and tie.

2nd Row. R, 3 d, join to center p of any large r of 1st row, 3 d, cl r, turn. * Ch, 5 d, 3 p sep by 2 d, 5 d. turn. R, 3 d, join to center p of next large r, 3 d, cl r, turn.

(Continued on page 8.)

(Continued from page 7.)

Repeat from * all around ending row with ch, 5 d, 3 p sep by 2 d, 5 d, join, cut and tie.

3rd Row. R, 3 d, join to 6th p to left of center small r at end of work, 3 d, cl r, turn. * Ch, 5 d, 3 p sep by 2 d, 5 d, turn. R, 3 d, skip 1 p, join to next p of same ch, 3 d, cl r, turn. Ch, 5 d, 3 p sep by 2 d, 5 d, turn. R, 3 d, join to next p of next ch, 3 d, cl r, turn. Repeat from * twice Ch, 5 d, 3 p sep by 2 d, 5 d, turn. R, 3 d, skip 1 p of same ch, join to next p, 3 d, cl r, turn. * Ch, 5 d, 3 p sep by 2 d, 5 d, turn. R, 3 d, join to center p of next ch, 3 d, cl r, turn. Repeat from * 14 times. * Ch, 5 d, 3 p sep by 2 d, 5 d, turn. R, 3 d, join to 1st p of next ch, 3 d, cl r, turn. Ch, 5 d, 3 p sep by 2 d, 5 d, turn. R, 3 d, skip 1 p of same ch, join to next p of same ch, 3 d, cl r, turn. Repeat from * 3 times. * Ch, 5 d, 3 p sep by 2 d, 5 d, turn. R, 3 d, join to center p of next ch, 3 d, cl r, turn. Repeat from * 14 times. Ch, 5 d, 3 p sep by 2 d, 5 d, join, tie and cut.

4th Row. R, 3 d, join to center p of any ch of 3rd row, 3 d, cl r, turn. * Ch, 5 d, 3 p sep by 2 d, 5 d, turn. R, 3 d, join to center p of next ch, 3 d, cl r, turn. Repeat from * all around ending row with ch, 5 d, 3 p sep by 2 d, 5 d, join, cut and tie.

5th Row. R, 2 d, join to 9th p to left side of center small r at end of work, 2 d, cl r, turn. Ch, 6 d, turn. R, 3 d, p, 2 d, 3 p sep by 1 d, 2 d, p, 3 d, cl r, turn. * Ch, 6 d, turn. R, 2 d, skip 1 p, join to next p of same ch, 2 d, cl r, turn. Ch, 6 d, turn. R, 3 d, p, 2 d, 3 p sep by 1 d, 2 d, p, 3 d, cl r, turn. Ch, 6 d, turn. R, 2 d, join to next p of next ch, 2 d, cl r, turn. Repeat from * 4 times. Ch, 6 d, turn. R, 3 d, p, 2 d, 3 p sep by 1 d, 2 d, p, 3 d, cl r, turn. Ch, 6 d, turn. R, 2 d, skip 1 p, join to next p of same ch, 2 d, cl r, turn. * Ch, 6 d, turn. R, 3 d, p, 2 d, 3 p sep by 1 d, 2 d, p, 3 d, cl r, turn. Ch, 6 d, turn. R, 2 d, join to center p of next ch, 2 d, cl r, turn. Repeat from * 16 times. * Ch, 6 d, turn. R, 3 d, p, 2 d, 3 p sep by 1 d, 2 d, p, 3 d, cl r, turn. Ch, 6 d, turn. R, 2 d, join to 1st p of next ch, 2 d, cl r, turn. Ch, 6 d, turn. R, 3 d, p, 2 d, 3 p sep by 1 d, 2 d, p, 3 d, cl r, turn. Ch, 6 d, turn. R, 2 d, skip 1 p, join to next p of same ch, 2 d, cl r, turn. Repeat from * 5 times. * Ch, 6 d, turn. R, 3 d, p, 2 d, 3 p sep by 1 d, 2 d, p, 3 d, cl r, turn. Ch, 6 d, turn. R, 2 d, join to center p of next ch, 2 d, cl r, turn. Repeat from * 16 times. Ch, 6 d, turn. R, 3 d, p, 2 d, 3 p sep by 1 d, 2 d, p, 3 d, cl r, turn. Ch, 6 d, join, cut and tie.

6th Row. R, 3 d, p, 2 d, p, 1 d, join to center p of any r of previous row, 1 d, p, 2 d, p, 3 d, cl r, turn. * Ch, 5 d, 5 p sep by 1 d, 5 d, turn. R, 3 d, p, 2 d, p, 1 d, join to center p of next r, 1 d, p, 2 d, p, 3 d, cl r, turn. Repeat from * all around ending row with ch, 5 d, 5 p sep by 1 d, 5 d, join, cut and tie.

7th Row. R, 4 d, 2 p sep by 2 d, 2 d, cl r. * R, 3 d, join to last p of small r, 2 d, 5 p sep by 1 d, 2 d, p, 3 d, cl r. R, 2 d, join to last p of large r, 2 d, p, 4 d, cl r, turn. Ch, 5 d, 2 p sep by 1 d, 1 d, join to center p of any ch of previous row, 1 d, 2 p sep by 1 d, 5 d, turn. R, 4 d, join to free p of last small r, 2 d, p, 2 d, cl r. Repeat from * all around ending row with R, 3 d, join to last p of small r, 2 d, 5 p sep by 1 d, 3 d, p, 3 d, cl r. R, 2 d, join to last p of large r, 2 d, join to corresponding p of 1st r, 4 d, cl r, turn. Ch, 5 d, 2 p sep by 1 d, 1 d, join to center p of ch in previous row, 1 d, 2 p sep by 1 d, 5 d, join, cut and tie.

8th Row. R, 4 d, join to center p of center r at end of work, 4 d, cl r, turn. Ch, 15 d, p, 10 d, turn. R, 4 d, p, 3 d, 5 p sep by 1 d, 3 d, p, 4 d, cl r. R, 4 d, join to last p of last r made, 3 d, 5 p sep by 1 d, 3 d, p, 4 d, cl r, turn. * Ch, 15 d, turn. R, 3 d, 3 p sep by 3 d, 3 d, cl r. R, 4 d, join to last p of last r made, 3 d, 5 p sep by 1 d, 3 d, p, 4 d, cl r. R, 3 d, join to last p of last r made, 3 d, 2 p sep by 3 d, 3 d, cl r, turn. Ch, 15 d, turn. R, 4 d, p, 3 d, 5 p sep by 1 d, 3 d, p, 4 d, cl r. R, 4 d, join to last p of last r made, 3 d, 5 p sep by 1 d, 3 d, p, 4 d, cl r, turn. Ch, 10 d, join to p of opposite ch, 15 d, turn. R, 4 d, skip 1 large r of previous row, join to center p of next r, 4 d, cl r, turn. Ch, 15 d, p, 10 d, turn. R, 4 d, p, 3 d, 4 p sep by 1 d, 1 d, join to corresponding p of corresponding r, 3 d, p, 4 d, cl r. R, 4 d, join to last p of last r, 3 d, join to corresponding p of next corresponding r, 1 d, 4 p sep by 1 d, 3 d, p, 4 d, cl r. Repeat from * in same manner all around ending row with ch, 15 d, turn. R, 3 d, 3 p sep by 3 d, 3 d, cl r. R, 4 d, join to last p of last r made, 3 d, 5 p sep by 1 d, 3 d, p, 4 d, cl r. R, 3 d, join to last p of last r made, 3 d, 2 p sep by 3 d, 3 d, cl r, turn. Ch, 15 d, turn. R, 4 d, p, 3 d, 4 p sep by 1 d, 1 d, join to corresponding p of corresponding r, 3 d, p, 4 d, cl r. R, 4 d, join to last p of last r, 3 d, join to corresponding p of corresponding r, 1 d, 4 p sep by 1 d, 3 d, p, 4 d, cl r, turn. Ch, 10 d, join to corresponding p of opposite ch, 15 d, join, tie and cut.

COBWEB DOILY

Materials: Clark's O.N.T. or J. & P. Coats Mercerized Crochet, size 30, 1 ball.

A shuttle.

When completed, doily measures about 4 inches in diameter.

Starting at center, make r of 5 ds, 8 p's sep. by 6 ds, 1 ds, cl. Tie securely and cut off. **1st rnd:** R of 3 ds, p, 3 ds, p, 3 ds, p, 3 ds, join to p of center r, 3 ds, p, 3 ds, p, 3 ds, p, 3 ds, cl. * Rw, attach ball thread, ch of 5 ds, p, 5 ds, p, 5 ds, p, 5 ds. Rw, r of 3 ds, p, 3 ds, sk last p of 1st r, join to next p, 3 ds, p, 3 ds, join to next p of center r, 3 ds, p, 3 ds, p, 3 ds, p, 3 ds, cl. Repeat from * around, joining last r to 1st and 7th r's, and joining last ch to tip of 1st r. Tie securely and cut off. **2nd rnd:** * R of 3 ds, 7 p's sep. by 3 ds, 3 ds, cl. Rw, ch of 3 ds, p, 3 ds, p, 3 ds, p, 4 ds, join to center p of ch of 1st rnd, 4 ds, p, 3 ds, p, 3 ds, p, 3 ds. Rw. Repeat from * around, joining last ch to 1st r made. Tie securely and cut off. **3rd rnd:** R of 4 ds, 7 p's sep. by 3 ds, 4 ds, cl. Rw, ch of 4 ds, sk 2 p's of r of 2nd rnd, join to next p, 4 ds. * Rw, r of 4 ds, join to last p of 1st r, 3 ds, 6 p's sep. by 3 ds, 4 ds, cl. Rw, ch of 4 ds, join to next p of same r of 2nd rnd, 4 ds. Rw, r of 4 ds, join to last p of previous r, 3 ds, 6 p's sep. by 3 ds, 4 ds, cl. Rw, ch of 4 ds, join to next p of same r of 2nd rnd, 4 ds. Rw, r of 4 ds, join to last p of previous r, 4 ds, cl. Rw, ch of 4 ds, join to next p of r of 2nd rnd, 4 ds, 5 p's sep. by 3 ds, 4 ds, join to 2nd p of next r of 2nd rnd, 4 ds. Rw, r of 4 ds, p, 3 ds, p, 3 ds, sk 2 p's of last r made, join to next p, 3 ds, 4 p's sep. by 3 ds, 4 ds, cl. Rw, ch of 4 ds, join to next p of same r of 2nd rnd, 4 ds. Repeat from * around, joining last r to 1st r made. Tie securely and cut off.

TATTED EDGINGS

**Materials Required—AMERICAN THREAD COMPANY
"STAR" MERCERIZED TATTING COTTON
White or Colors**

No. 3002

Use 1 Shuttle and a Ball.

1—75 Yd. Ball will make about 1½ Yds. of Lace.

R, 6 d, p, 6 d, close r. Work 4 more rings. * Ch, 6 d, 3 p sep by 2 d, 6 d, p, 6 d, join to p of 4th r made, 4 d, turn. R, 2 d, 7 p sep by 2 d, 2 d, close r, turn. Ch, 4 d, p, 6 d, join to p on opposite ch, 6 d, 3 p sep by 2 d, 6 d, turn. R, 6 d, p, 6 d, close r. R, 6 d, join to p of ch, 6 d, close r. Work 3 more rings of 6 d, p, 6 d and repeat from * for length desired.

No. 3003

Use 2 Shuttles or 1 Ball and 1 Shuttle.

1—75 Yd. Ball will make about 1⅛ Yds. of Lace.

L R, 1 d, 12 p, sep by 1 d, 1 d, close r. Ch, 4 d, 3 p sep by 2 d, 4 d. * S R, 4 d, join to 10th p of large r, 4 d, close r. Ch. 4 d, 7 p sep by 2 d, 4 d. S R, 4 d, join to same p of large r, 4 d, close r. Ch, 4 d, 3 p sep by 2 d, 4 d, skip 2 p of large r, join to next p, 5 d. S R, 4 d, p, 4 d, close r. Ch, 5 d. L R, 1 d, 12 p, sep by 1 d, 1 d, close r. Ch, 4 d, p, 2 d, join to center p of opposite ch, 2 d, p, 4 d, repeat from * for desired length.

Heading. S R, 4 d, join to 4th p of large r, 4 d, close r. Ch, 4 d, 3 p sep by 2 d, 4 d, join to s r of 1st row. Ch, 4 d, 3 p sep by 2 d, 4 d, repeat from beginning across row.

No. 3004

Use 1 Shuttle and a Ball.

1—75 Yd. Ball will make about 1¼ Yds. of Lace.

R, 3 d, 3 p sep by 3 d, 3 d, close r, turn. Ch, 4 d, 3 p sep by 2 d, 4 d, turn. * R, 3 d, join to last p of 1st r, 3 d, p, 3 d, p, 3 d, close r, turn. Ch, 4 d, 3 p sep by 2 d, 4 d, turn. R, 3 d, p, 3 d, join to center p of last r, 3 d, p, 3 d, close r, turn. Ch, 4 d, 3 p sep by 2 d, 4 d, turn. R, 3 d, join to last p of last r made, 3 d, join to center p of 1st r made, 3 d, p, 3 d, close r, turn. Ch, 4 d, 4 p sep by 2 d, 5 d, turn. R, 6 d, join to 1st p of ch, 6 d, close r. R, 6 d, join to 3rd p of same ch, 6 d, close r. Work 2 more r of 6 d, p, 6 d, turn. Ch, 5 d, join to 1st p of upper ch, 2 d, 3 p sep by 2 d, 4 d, turn. R, 3 d, 3 p sep by 3 d, 3 d, close r, turn. Ch, 4 d, join to p of last r made, 2 d, p, 2 d, join to p of next r, 4 d, turn, repeat from * for desired length.

No. 3005

Use 2 Shuttles or 1 Shuttle and 1 Ball.

3—75 Yd. Balls will make about 1 Yd. of Lace.

Heading. 1st Row. L R, 5 d, 5 p sep by 2 d, 5 d, close r, ¼ inch space, turn. * S R, 4 d, long p, 4 d, close r. ¼ inch space, turn. L R, 5 d, join to last p of 1st large r, 2 d, 4 p sep by 2 d, 5 d, close r. ¼ inch space, turn. S R, 4 d, join to long p of last s r, 4 d, close r. ¼ inch space, turn. L R, 4 d, join to last p of last large r, 2 d, 4 p sep by 2 d, 5 d, close r. Repeat from * for desired length, tie and cut. Repeat 1st row joining 2 s r in long p of s r in 1st row.

Medallion. R, 1 d, 14 p sep by 1 d, 1 d, close r, tie and cut thread. L R, 6 d, 5 p sep by 2 d, 6 d, close r. ¼ inch space, turn. S R, 4 d, join to p of center r, 4 d, close r. ¼ inch space, turn. * L R, 6 d, join to 5th p of last r, 4 p sep by 2 d, 6 d, close r. ¼ inch space, turn. S R, 4 d, join to next p of center r, 4 d, close r. ¼ inch space, turn and repeat from * joining center p of 3 large rings to 3 large rings of heading.

Second Medallion is joined to 1st medallion in center picots of 2 large rings and to heading at center p of 3 large rings, leaving 1 ring on medallions, 2 rings on heading free between joinings.

No. 3006

Use 2 Shuttles or 1 Shuttle and a Ball.

1—75 Yd. Ball will make about 2 Yds. of Lace.

R, 3 d, 3 p sep by 3 d, 3 d, close r. Ch, 3 d, 3 p sep by 3 d, 3 d, * join to center p of r, 3 d, turn. R, 1 d, 8 p sep by 1 d, 1 d close r, turn. Ch, 3 d. R, 3 d, 3 p sep by 3 d, 3 d, close r. Ch, 3 d, join to p on opposite ch, 3 d, p, 3 d, p, 3 d, repeat from * for desired length.

No. 3007

Use 1 Shuttle and a Ball.

1—75 Yd. Ball will make about 1¼ Yds. of Lace.

R, 2 d, 7 p sep by 2 d, 2 d, close r. Ch, 4 d, p, * 6 d, p, 2 d, p, 2 d, p, 6 d, p, 6 d, join to center p of r, 6 d, turn. R, 4 d, 7 p sep by 2 d, 4 d, close r. Ch, 4 d, turn. R, 4 d, join to last p of last r, 2 d, 9 p sep by 2 d, 4 d, close r. Ch, 4 d, turn. R, 4 d, join to last p of last r made, 2 d, 6 p sep by 2 d, 4 d, close r, turn. Ch, 6 d, turn. R, 4 d, 7 p sep by 2 d, 4 d, close r, turn. Ch, 6 d, join to p on opposite ch, 6 d, 3 p sep by 2 d, 6 d, p, 6 d, join to center p of last r made, 4 d, turn. R, 2 d, 7 p sep by 2 d, 2 d, close r, turn. Ch, 4 d, turn. R, 2 d, 7 p sep by 2 d, 2 d, close r. Ch, 6 d, join to p on opposite ch, repeat from * for desired length.

No. 3008

Use 1 Shuttle and 1 Ball.

1—75 Yd. Ball will make about 2 Yds. of Edging.

R, 4 d, p, 4 d, p, 4 d, p, 4 d, close r. Ch, 6 d, p, 6 d, p, 2 d, p, 2 d, p, 6 d, p, 6 d, join to base of r, turn work. * Ch, 5 d, p, 2 d, p, 2 d, p, 5 d, turn work. R, 4 d, join to p of ch, 4 d, p, 4 d, p, 4 d, close r, turn work. Ch, 4 d, p, 2 d, p, 2 d, p, 4 d, turn work. R, 4 d, p, 4 d, p, 4 d, p, 4 d,

close r. Ch, 4 d, join to side p of r, 4 d, p, 2 d, p, 2 d, p, 4 d, join to base of ring and repeat from * for length desired.

No. 3009

Use 1 Shuttle and a Ball.

1—75 Yd. Ball will make about 1¼ Yds. of Lace.

R, 4 d, p, 4 d, p, 4 d, close r. R, 4 d, join to side p of 1st r, 4 d, p, 2 d, p, 2 d, p, 4 d, p, 4 d, close r. R, 4 d, join to side p of r, 4 d, p, 4 d, p, 4 d, close r. Ch, 6 d, p, 2 d, p, 2 d, p, 6 d, p, 6 d, join to center p of 2nd r, 6 d. R, 2 d, 6 p

sep by 2 d, 2 d, close r. Join thread to 1st p. R, 3 d, p, 3 d, * join to center p of 1st r made, 3 d, p, 3 d, close r. Join to 2nd p of center r. R, 3 d, join to side p of small r, 3 d, p, 3 d, p, 3 d, close r. Repeat from * until there are 6 small rings, turn work. Ch, 6 d, p, 6 d, join to p on opposite ch, 6 d, p, 2 d, p, 2 d, p, 6 d, turn work. R, 4 d, p, 4 d, p, 4 d, p, 4 d, close r. R, 4 d, join to side p of last r made, 4 d, p, 2 d, join to p of ch, 2 d, p, 4 d, p, 4 d, close r. R, 4 d, join to side p of last r made, 4 d, join to center p of last small r made, 4 d, p, 4 d, close r. Repeat from beginning joining next ring to previous ring at side p.

No. 1   No. 2   No. 3

LACE ELEGANCE

Materials Required for TATTED Medallions—AMERICAN THREAD COMPANY "STAR" MERCERIZED TATTING COTTON, White or Colors

1—75 Yd. Ball will make all three motifs.

No. 1

1 Shuttle and 1 Ball.

R, 2 d, 5 p sep by 2 d, 2 d, cl r. Ch, 2 d, 5 sep by 2 d, 2 d. * R, 2 d, p, 2 d, join to 4th p of last r, 2 d, 3 p sep by 2 d, 2 d, cl r. Ch, 2 d, 5 p sep by 2 d, 2 d, repeat from * until there are 8 rings in center, tie and cut.

2nd Row. R, 4 d, p, 3 d, 5 p sep by 2 d, 3 d, p, 4 d, **cl r.** R, 4 d, join to last p of last r, 3 d, 7 p sep by 2 d, 3 d, p, 4 d, cl r. R, 4 d, join to last p of last r, 3 d, 5 p sep by 2 d, 3 d, p, 4 d, cl r. Ch, 4 d, p, 8 d, join to center p of any scallop, 8 d, p, 4 d. * R, 4 d, p, 3 d, p, 2 d, join to 4th p of last r, 2 d, p, 2 d, p, 3 d, p, 4 d, cl r. R, 4 d, join to last p of last r, 3 d, 7 p sep by 2 d, 3 d, p, 4 d, cl r. R, 4 d, join to last p of last r, 3 d, 5 p sep by 2 d, 3 d, p, 4 d, cl r. Ch, 4 d, join to p of last ch, 8 d, join to center p of next scallop, 8 d, p, 4 d, repeat from * all around, tie and cut.

No. 2

1 Shuttle and 1 Ball.

R, 3 d, 5 p sep by 3 d, 3 d, cl r. R, 3 d, join to last p of last r, 3 d, 6 p sep by 3 d, 3 d, cl r. R, 3 d, join to last p of last r, 3 d, 4 p sep by 3 d, 3 d, cl r. Ch, 12 d, p, 12 d. * R, 3 d, p, 3 d, join to 4th p of last r, 3 d, 3 p sep by 3 d, 3 d, cl r. R, 3 d, join to last p of last r, 3 d, 6 p sep by 3 d, 3 d, cl r. R, 3 d, join to last p of last r, 3 d, 4 p sep by 3 d, 3 d, cl r. Ch, 6 d, p, 6 d, repeat from * twice joining the 4th p of last r to 2nd p of 1st r, tie and cut.

2nd Row. R, 3 d, p, 3 d, join to 2nd free p of corner r, 3 d, p, 3 d, cl r. Ch, 4 d, 7 p sep by 2 d, 4 d. R, 3 d, p, 3 d, skip 1 p, join to next p, 3 d, p, 3 d, cl r. Ch, 4 d, 5 p sep by 2 d, 4 d. R, 3 d, p, 3 d, join to center p of small r, 1 d, join to center p of next small r, 3 d, p, 3 d, cl r. Ch, 4 d, 5 p sep by 2 d, 4 d, repeat from beginning all around.

No. 3

1 Shuttle and 1 Ball.

R, 2 d, 5 p sep by 2 d, 2 d, cl r. * Ch, 4 d, p, 4 d, p, 4 d, p, 4 d. R, 2 d, p, 2 d, join to 4th p of previous r, 2 d, p, 2 d, p, 2 d, p, 2 d, cl r. Repeat from * 4 times. Ch, 4 d, p, 4 d, p, 4 d, p, 4 d, tie and cut.

2nd Row. R, 3 d, p, 3 d, join to p of 1st row, 3 d, p, 3 d, cl r. * Ch, 3 d, 4 p sep by 2 d, 3 d. R, 3 d, p, 3 d, join to next p of 1st row, 3 d, p, 3 d, cl r. Repeat from * all around. Ch, 3 d, 4 p sep by 2 d, 3 d, tie and cut.

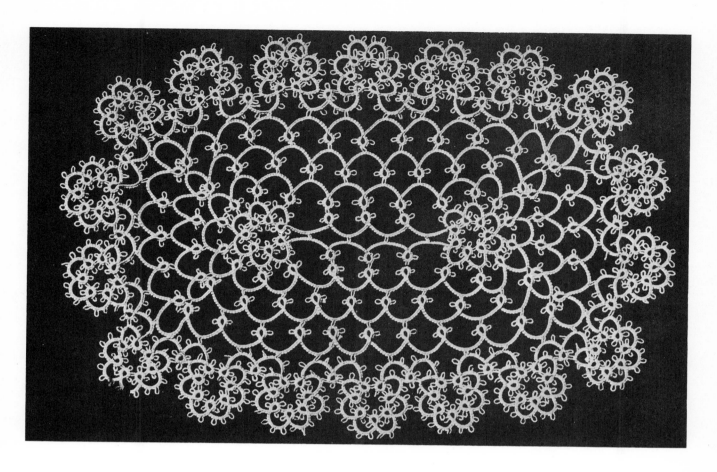

OCCASIONAL DOILY

Materials: CLARK'S O.N.T. or J. & P. COATS MERCERIZED CROCHET, size 10, 2 balls of White or Ecru.

Completed doily measures 7½ x 11 inches.

1st rnd: Starting at center, make r of 2 ds, 5 p's sep. by 2 ds, 2 ds, cl. Rw, ch of 3 ds, 3 p's sep. by 3 ds, 3 ds. Rw, r of 2 ds, p, 2 ds, skip 1 p of last r, join to next p, 2 ds, p, 2 ds, p, 2 ds, p, 2 ds, cl. Continue thus until 6 r's and 6 ch's are made. Rw, r of 2 ds, p, 2 ds, skip 1 p of previous r, join to next p, 2 ds, p, 2 ds. Join to 2nd p of 1st r, 2 ds, p, 2 ds, cl (a motif completed at one end of 1st rnd). Ch of 8 ds, p, 8 ds. * Rw, r of 3 ds, 3 p's sep. by 3 ds, 3 ds, cl. Rw, ch of 8 ds, p, 8 ds. Repeat from * 2 more times. Make a motif to correspond with 1st motif. Ch of 8 ds, join to p of adjacent ch, 8 ds. ** Rw, r of 3 ds, 3 p's sep. by 3 ds, 3 ds, cl. Rw, ch of 8 ds, join to p of adjacent ch, 8 ds. Repeat from ** across, joining last ch to base of 1st r. Tie ends and cut. **2nd rnd:** R of 3 ds, p, 3 ds, join to center p of 1st ch of motif, 3 ds, p, 3 ds, cl. Rw, ch of 8 ds, p, 8 ds. Rw, r of 3 ds, p, 3 ds, join to center p of next ch, 3 ds, p, 3 ds, cl. Rw, ch of 8 ds, p, 8 ds. Rw, r of 3 ds, p, 3 ds, join to 1st p of next ch, 3 ds, p, 3 ds, cl. Rw, ch of 8 ds, p, 8 ds. Rw, r of 3 ds, p, 3 ds, skip 1 p, join to next p of same ch, 3 ds, p, 3 ds, cl. Rw, ch of 4 ds, p, 8 ds, p, 4 ds. Rw, r of 3 ds, p, 3 ds, join to 1st p of next ch, 3 ds, p, 3 ds, cl. Rw, ch of 8 ds, p, 8 ds. Rw, r of 3 ds, p, 3 ds, skip 1 p, join to next p of same ch, 3 ds, p, 3 ds, cl. Rw, ch of 8 ds, p, 8 ds. Rw, r of 3 ds, p, 3 ds, join to center p of next ch, 3 ds, p, 3 ds, cl. Rw, ch of 8 ds, p, 8 ds. Rw, r of 3 ds, p, 3 ds, join to center p of next ch, 3 ds, p, 3 ds, cl. Rw, ch of 8 ds, p, 8 ds. Rw, r of 3 ds, p, 3 ds, join to center p of next r, 3 ds, p, 3 ds, cl. Rw, ch of 8 ds, p, 8 ds. Rw, r of 3 ds, p, 3 ds, join to center p of next r, 3 ds, p, 3 ds, cl. Rw, ch of 8 ds, p, 8 ds. Rw, r of 3 ds, p, 3 ds, join to center p of ch on 2nd motif, 3 ds, p, 3 ds, cl. Continue around motif as before and across ch to 1st r made. Tie and cut. **3rd rnd:** R of 3 ds, p, 3 ds, join to p of ch preceding 1st r joined to motif on 2nd rnd, 3 ds, p, 3 ds, cl. * Rw, ch of 8 ds, p, 8 ds. Rw, r of 3 ds, p, 3 ds, join to center p of next ch (motif), 3 ds, p, 3 ds, cl. Repeat from * 2 more times. Rw, ch of 8 ds, p, 8 ds. Rw, r of 3 ds, p, 3 ds, join to same p as last r, 3 ds, p, 3 ds, cl. Rw, ch of 8 ds, p, 8 ds. Rw, r of 3 ds, p, 3 ds, join to 1st p of next ch, 3 ds, p, 3 ds, cl. Rw, ch of 8 ds, p, 8 ds. Rw, r of 3 ds, p, 3 ds, join to next p of same ch, 3 ds, p, 3 ds, cl. Rw, ch of 8 ds, p, 8 ds. Rw, r of 3 ds, p, 3 ds, join to p of next ch, 3 ds, p, 3 ds, cl. Rw, ch of 8 ds, p, 8 ds. Rw, r of 3 ds, p, 3 ds, join to same p as last r (ch between these 2 r's forms corner), 3 ds, p, 3 ds, cl. ** Rw, ch of 8 ds, p, 8 ds, rw. R of 3 ds, p, 3 ds, join to next p of next ch, 3 ds, p, 3 ds, cl. Repeat from ** 7 more times. Work around motif to correspond with opposite end and complete rnd, joining last ch to base of 1st p. Tie and cut. **4th rnd:** R of 3 ds, p, 3 ds, join to p of ch on 3rd rnd, 3 ds, p, 3 ds, cl. Rw, ch of 8 ds, p, 8 ds. Continue thus around, but at corners make r of 3 ds, p, 3 ds, join to p on ch of 1st corner, 3 ds, p, 3 ds, cl. Rw, ch of 8 ds, p, 8 ds, p, 8 ds. Rw, r of 3 ds, p, 3 ds, join to same p as last r, 3 ds, p, 3 ds, cl. Tie and cut.

EDGING . . . R of 2 ds, 5 p's sep. by 2 ds, 2 ds, cl. ** Rw, ch of 4 ds, p, 4 ds, join to p of ch on previous rnd, 4 ds, p, 4 ds. Rw, r of 2 ds, 5 p's sep. by 2 ds, 2 ds, cl. Rw, ch of 3 ds, p, 3 ds, skip 1 p of adjacent r, join to next p, 3 ds, p, 3 ds. * Rw, r of 2 ds, p, 2 ds, skip 1 p of jacent ch, join to next p, 2 ds, 3 p's sep. by 2 ds, p, 2 ds, p, 2 ds, cl. Rw, ch of 3 ds, 3 p's sep. by 3 ds, 3 ds. Repeat from * until 7 r's are made, joining last r on both sides. Ch of 4 ds, p, 4 ds, join to p of next ch on previous rnd, 4 ds, p, 4 ds. Rw, r of 2 ds, p, 2 ds, skip 1 p of adjacent ch, join to next p, 2 ds, 3 p's sep. by 2 ds, 2 ds, cl. Repeat from ** around, making a motif at each corner and joining a ch at corner to each p of 2-p ch (18 motifs in the rnd). Tie ends and cut.

WHIP CREAM FRILL

TATTED DOILY

Materials Required—
AMERICAN THREAD COMPANY
"STAR" MERCERIZED CROCHET COTTON

1 175-yd. Ball White, Size 50.
1 Shuttle and 1 Ball.

Center. R, 4 d, 5 p sep by 3 d, 4 d, cl r, turn. Ch, 10 d, turn. Small R, 3 d, 3 p sep by 3 d, 3 d, cl r. * Large R, 4 d, join to last p of small r, 3 d, 4 p sep by 3 d, 4 d, cl r. Small R, 3 d, join to last p of large r, 3 d, 2 p sep by 3 d, 3 d, cl r. Ch, 10 d, turn. R, 4 d, p, 3 d, join to 4th p of center r, 3 d, 3 p sep by 3 d, 4 d, cl r, turn. Ch, 10 d. R, 3 d, 3 p sep by 3 d, 3 d, join to center p of 2nd small r of clover, 3 d, 3 p sep by 3 d, 3 d, cl r. R, 3 d, 7 p sep by 3 d, 3 d, cl r. Ch, 10 d, turn. R, 4 d, p, 3 d, join to 4th p of next center r, 3 d, 3 p sep by 3 d, 4 d, cl r, turn. Ch, 10 d. Small r, 3 d, p, 3 d, join to center p of large r, 3 d, p, 3 d, cl r. Repeat from * until there are 10 center rings tie and cut.

2nd Row—* R, 3 d, p, 3 d, join to free center p of 1st large r between clovers, 3 d, p, 3 d, cl r, turn. Ch, 12 d. R, 1 d, 9 long p sep by 1 d, 1 d, cl r. Ch, 12 d, turn. R, 3 d, p, 3 d, join to next free center p of next large r, 3 d, p, 3 d, cl r, turn. Ch, 12 d. R, 1 d, 9 long p sep by 1 d, 1 d, cl r. Ch, 12 d, turn, join to center p of large r of clover, turn. Ch, 12 d, R, 1 d, 9 long p sep by 1 d, 1 d, cl r. Ch, 12 d. Repeat from * 4 times, tie and cut.

3rd Row—R, 3 d, 3 p sep by 3 d, 3 d, cl r. * R, 4 d, join to 3rd p of r just made, 3 d, 4 p sep by 3 d, 4 d, cl r. R, 3 d, join to last p of r just made, 3 d, 2 p sep by 3 d, cl r, turn. Ch, 12 d, 3 p sep by 2 d, 12 d, turn. R, 4 d, join to center p of last r made, 2 d, 2 long p sep by 2 d, 2 d, join to center p of any r in 2nd row, 2 d, 3 long p sep by 2 d, 4 d, cl r, turn. Ch, 12 d, 3 p sep by 2 d, 12 d, turn. R, 3 d, p, 3 d, join to last p of last r made, 3 d, p, 3 d, cl r. Repeat from * in same manner all around, join, tie and cut.

4th Row—Small R, 3 d, 3 p sep by 3 d, 3 d, cl r. * Large R, 4 d, join to 3rd p of small r, 3 d, 6 p sep by 2 d, 4 d, cl r. Small R, 3 d, join to last p of large r, 3 d, 2 p sep by 3 d, 3 d, cl r. Ch, 12 d, p, 2 d, join to center p of ch in previous row, 2 d, p, 12 d. Small R, 3 d, p, 3 d, join to small r of 1st clover and repeat from * all around, join, tie and cut.

OUTSIDE MOTIF. R, 3 d, 5 p sep by 3 d, 3 d, cl r. Large r, 3 d, join to last p of last r, 3 d, 3 p sep by 2 d, 2 d, join to center p of any large r of 4th row, 2 d, 3 p sep by 2 d, 3 d, p, 3 d, cl r. R, 3 d, join to last p of last r, 3 d, 4 p sep by 3 d, 3 d, cl r, turn. * Ch, 8 d, p, 8 d. R, 3 d, p, 3 d, join to 4th p of last r, 3 d, 3 p sep by 3 d, 3 d, cl r. Large R, 3 d, join to last p of last r, 3 d, 7 p sep by 2 d, 3 d, p, 3 d, cl r. R, 3 d, join to last p of last r, 3 d, 4 p sep by 3 d, 3 d, cl r, turn. Repeat from * twice. Ch, 8 d, p, 8 d, tie and cut.

Work 14 more motifs in same manner joining to center p of every other r of 4th row and joining motifs at center p at sides of motifs as illustrated.

14

BREAD TRAY DOILY

Materials: CLARK'S O.N.T. or J. & P. COATS MERCERIZED CROCHET, size 10, 1 ball of White or Ecru.

6 square inches of linen.

Completed doily measures about 5½ x 10½ inches. Cut linen 4¾ x 5 inches, curving the 2 shorter sides as in illustration. Make narrow hem around all edges.

CENTER MOTIF . . . Tie shuttle and ball threads. R of 2 ds, 5 p's sep. by 2 ds, 2 ds, cl. * Rw, ch of 3 ds, 3 p's sep. by 3 ds, 3 ds. Rw, r of 2 ds, p, 2 ds, skip 1 p of previous r, join to next p, 2 ds, 3 p's sep. by 2 ds, 2 ds, cl. Repeat from * until 6 r's and 6 ch's are made. Rw, r of 2 ds, p, 2 ds, join to 4th p of previous r, 2 ds, p, 2 ds, join to 2nd p of 1st r, 2 ds, p, 2 ds, cl. Rw, ch of 3 ds, 3 p's sep. by 3 ds, 3 ds, join to base of 1st r. Tie ends and cut.

OUTER MOTIF . . . R of 2 ds, 5 p's sep. by 2 ds, 2 ds, cl. * Rw, ch of 3 ds, 3 p's sep. by 3 ds, 3 ds. Rw, r of 2 ds, p, 2 ds, join to 4th p of previous r, 2 ds, 3 p's sep. by 2 ds, 2 ds, cl. Rw, ch of 3 ds, 3 p's sep. by 3 ds, 3 ds. Rw, r of 2 ds, p, 2 ds, join to 4th p of previous r, 2 ds, 3 p's sep. by 2 ds, 2 ds, cl. Rw, ch of 4 ds, p, 4 ds, join to center p of 1st ch of center motif, 4 ds, p, 4 ds. R of 2 ds, 5 p's sep. by 2 ds, 2 ds, cl. Rw, ch of 3 ds, p, 3 ds, join to 4th p of adjacent r of outer row, 3 ds, p, 3 ds. Rw, r of 2 ds, p, 2 ds, join to 4th p of last r, 2 ds, 3 p's sep. by 2 ds, 2 ds, cl. Rw, ch of 3 ds, p, 3 ds, skip 1 p of 1st r made on outer row, join to next

p; 3 ds, p, 3 ds. Rw, r of 2 ds, p, 2 ds, join to 4th p of last r, 2 ds, 3 p's sep. by 2 ds, 2 ds, cl. Rw, ch of 3 ds, 3 p's sep. by 3 ds, 3 ds. Rw, r of 2 ds, p, continue around as for 1st motif until 6 r's and 6 ch's are made. Rw, r of 2 ds, p, 2 ds, join to 4th p of previous r, 2 ds, p, 2 ds, join to 2nd p of 1st r, 2 ds, p, 2 ds, cl. Rw, ch of 4 ds, p, 4 ds, join to center p of next ch of center motif, 4 ds, p, 4 ds. Rw, r of 2 ds, p, 2 ds, join to center p of last ch of outer motif; 2 ds, 3 p's sep. by 2 ds, 2 ds, cl. Rw, ch of 4 ds, p, 4 ds, join to 1st p of next ch of center motif, 4 ds, p, 4 ds. R of 2 ds, 5 p's sep. by 2 ds, 2 ds, cl. Rw, ch of 3 ds, p, 3 ds, join to 4th p of adjacent r, 3 ds, p, 3 ds. Continue around as for 1st motif until 6 r's and 6 ch's are made. Rw, r of 2 ds, p, 2 ds, join to 4th p of previous r, 2 ds, p, 2 ds, join to 2nd p of 1st r, 2 ds, p, 2 ds, cl. Ch of 4 ds, p, 4 ds, join to 3rd p of same ch of center motif, 4 ds, p, 4 ds. Rw, r of 2 ds, p, 2 ds, join to center p of adjacent ch, 2 ds, 3 p's sep. by 2 ds, 2 ds, cl. Rw, ch of 4 ds, p, 4 ds, join to center p of next ch of center motif, 4 ds, p, 4 ds. R of 2 ds, 5 p's sep. by 2 ds, 2 ds, cl. Rw, ch of 3 ds, p, 3 ds, join to 4th p of adjacent r, 3 ds, p, 3 ds. Rw, r of 2 ds, p, 2 ds, join to 4th p of previous r, 2 ds, 3 p's sep. by 2 ds, 2 ds, cl. Continue as for 1st motif until 6 ch's and 6 r's are made. Rw, r of 2 ds, p, 2 ds, join to 4th p of previous r, 2 ds, p, 2 ds, join to 2nd p of 1st r, 2 ds, p, 2 ds, cl. Ch of 4 ds, p, 4 ds, join to center p of next ch of center motif; 4 ds, p, 4 ds. Rw, r of 2 ds, p, 2 ds, join to center p of adjacent ch of outer motif, 2 ds, 3 p's sep. by 2 ds, 2 ds, cl. Rw, ch of 3 ds, 3 p's sep. by 3 ds, 3 ds.

Rw, r of 2 ds, p, 2 ds, join to 4th p of previous r, 2 ds, 3 p's sep. by 2 ds, 2 ds, cl. Rw, ch of 3 ds, 3 p's sep. by 3 ds, 3 ds. Rw, r of 2 ds, p, 2 ds, join to 4th p of previous r, 2 ds, p, 2 ds, join to center p of adjacent ch of outer motif; 2 ds, p, 2 ds, cl. Rw, ch of 3 ds, 3 p's sep. by 3 ds, 3 ds. Rw, r of 2 ds, p, 2 ds, join to center p of next ch, 2 ds, 3 p's sep. by 2 ds, 2 ds, cl. Rw, ch of 3 ds, 3 p's sep. by 3 ds, 3 ds. Rw, r of 2 ds, p, 2 ds, join to 4th p of previous r, 2 ds, 3 p's sep. by 2 ds, 2 ds, cl. Rw, ch of 3 ds, 3 p's sep. by 3 ds, 3 ds. Rw, r of 2 ds, p, 2 ds, join to 4th p of last r, 2 ds, p, 2 ds, join to center p of next ch, 2 ds, p, 2 ds, cl. Rw, ch of 3 ds, 3 p's sep. by 3 ds, 3 ds. Rw, r of 2 ds, p, 2 ds, join to center p of next ch, 2 ds, 3 p's sep. by 2 ds, 2 ds, cl. Rw, ch of 3 ds, 3 p's sep. by 3 ds, 3 ds. Rw, r of 2 ds, p, 2 ds, join to 4th p of previous r, 2 ds, 3 p's sep. by 2 ds, 2 ds, cl. Rw, ch of 3 ds, 3 p's sep. by 3 ds, 3 ds. Rw, r of 2 ds, p, 2 ds, join to 4th p of previous r, 2 ds, p, 2 ds, join to center p of 1st free ch on next motif, 2 ds, p, 2 ds, cl, rw. Ch of 3 ds, 3 p's sep. by 3 ds, 3 ds, rw. R of 2 ds, p, 2 ds, join to center p of next ch, 2 ds, 3 p's sep. by 2 ds, 2 ds, cl. Rw, ch of 3 ds, 5 p's sep. by 3 ds, 3 ds. Rw, r of 2 ds, p, 2 ds, join to 4th p of previous r, 2 ds, 3 p's sep. by 2 ds, 2 ds, cl. Rw, ch of 3 ds, 5 p's sep. by 3 ds, 3 ds. Rw, r of 2 ds, p, 2 ds, join to 4th p of previous r, 2 ds, p, 2 ds, join to center p of next ch, 2 ds, p, 2 ds, cl. Work along remainder of side to correspond with opposite side. Rw, ch of 3 ds, 3 p's sep. by 3 ds, 3 ds. Rw, r of 3 ds, 3 p's sep. by 3 ds, 3 ds, cl. Continue thus until 9 ch's and 8 r's are made. This completes one half of doily. Work other half to correspond. Sew lace to linen.

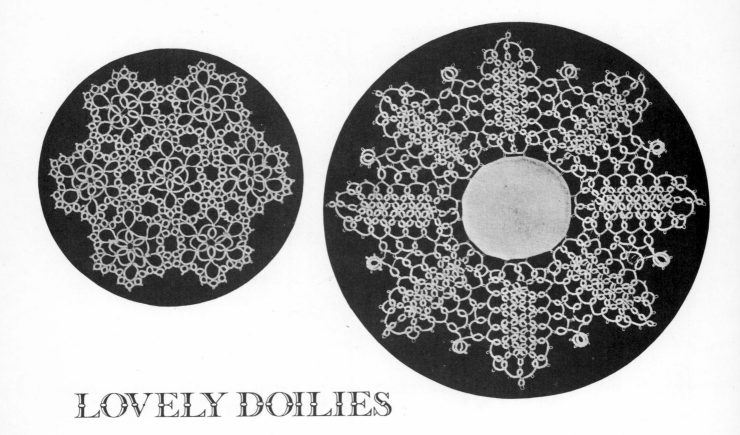

LOVELY DOILIES

Left　　　　**Materials:** Clark's O.N.T. or J. & P. Coats Mercerized Crochet, size 30, 1 ball of White, Ecru, or any color.

Completed doily measures about 7 inches in diameter. Tie shuttle and ball threads. Lr of 12 ds, lp (⅜ inch), 12 ds, cl. Rw, ch of 10 ds, sr of 8 ds, p, 4 ds, p, 4 ds, cl. ** Ch of 6 ds. * Sr of 4 ds, join to last p of previous sr, 4 ds, p, 4 ds, p, 4 ds, cl. Ch of 6 ds. Repeat from * until 4 sr's are made. Ch of 6 ds. Sr of 4 ds, join to last p of previous sr, 4 ds, p, 8 ds, cl. Ch of 10 ds, join to base of lr. Ch of 16 ds, rw. Lr of 12 ds, join to p of previous lr, 12 ds, cl. Rw, ch of 10 ds, r of 8 ds, join to p of last sr on ch, 4 ds, p, 4 ds, cl. Repeat from ** until six 5-sr ch's are made, taking care to join last p of last sr to p of 1st sr made on 1st ch. Make ch of 16 ds, join to base of lr first made. Tie ends and cut. Work 2nd medallion as far as 3rd sr of 3rd group. Join this sr to 3rd sr of 1st medallion. Join next sr of 2nd medallion to 4th sr of 1st medallion. Finish group and begin next group. Join 2nd sr of this group to 2nd sr of next group of 1st medallion. Join 3rd sr to 3rd sr of 1st medallion. Join 3rd medallion to 2 sr's of 1st medallion, to 2nd sr of next group; 3rd sr is joined to joining of 2 sr's. Join next sr, finish group and begin next group. Join 2nd and 3rd sr's of this group as usual, and finish medallion.

Right　　　　**Materials:** Clark's O.N.T. or J. & P. Coats Mercerized Crochet, size 20, 2 balls of White or Ecru.

Completed doily measures about 10 inches in diameter.

MOTIF . . . All rings are made in same way. R of 5 ds, p, 5 ds, cl. Make another r like this, rw. Make another sr, rw. Make another sr, rw. Make another sr, joining p to p of adjacent r (3rd r). Make another r, rw. Make another r, joining to adjacent r (4th r). Make another r, rw. Make another r, joining p to p of adjacent r (6th r). Make another r, rw. Make another r, joining p to adjacent r (8th r). Continue thus until there are 10 r's on each side of strip, not counting 1st r (the last r is a joined r); rw. Make another r (corner r), rw. Make another r, joining to adjacent 2 r's already joined, thus starting 2nd side of motif, rw. Make 2 more r's, rw. Make another r, joining to the 3 r's already joined. Make another r, joining to the following 2 r's already joined, rw. Join next r to last r with free p. Make another r, rw. Make another r, joining to 3 r's already joined. Continue thus along side until 5 squares are completed across center. Tie ends and cut. Tie shuttle and ball threads. R of 5 ds, join to corner r, 5 ds, cl. Rw, ch of 5 ds, p, 5 ds, rw. R of 5 ds, join to same p as last r, 5 ds, cl. Rw, ch of 5 ds, p, 5 ds, rw. R of 5 ds, join to center p at end, 5 ds, cl. Rw and make another r like this. Ch of 5 ds, p, 5 ds. Rw, r of 5 ds, join to p of r of next corner, 5 ds, cl. Rw, ch as before. Rw, r of 5 ds, join in same p as last r, 5 ds, cl. * Rw, ch as before. Rw, r of 5 ds, join to p where 2 r's were already joined, 5 ds, cl. Repeat from * 3 more times. Rw, ch as before. Now work other half of this rnd to correspond with first half. Tie ends and cut. Make 7 more motifs like this, joining the corner ch to corner p of previous motif and the following ch to adjacent p of ch on previous motif; also join the last motif to 1st motif, as well as to 7th motif.

FILL-IN MOTIFS . . . Tie threads. R of 9 ds, skip corner ch and the following ch on long side, join to next ch, 9 ds, cl. Rw, ch of 5 ds, p, 5 ds. Rw, r of 7 ds, join to p of next ch, 7 ds, cl. Rw, ch of 7 ds, rw. R of 5 ds, join to next ch, 5 ds, cl. R of 5 ds, join to p of adjacent ch on next motif; 5 ds, cl. Rw, ch of 7 ds. Rw, r of 7 ds, join to next ch, 7 ds, cl. Rw, ch of 5 ds, join to p of adjacent ch, 5 ds. Rw, r of 9 ds, join to p of next ch on 2nd motif, 9 ds, cl. Rw, ch of 7 ds. Rw, r of 9 ds, p, 9 ds, cl. Rw, ch of 5 ds, p, 5 ds, p, 4 ds, join to p of previous r, 4 ds, p, 5 ds, p, 5 ds, join to base of r (thus forming another r around previous r). Rw, 7 ds, join to base of 1st r made. Tie and cut. Fill in sps between all other r's in same way. Place lace over linen to form a circle and pin in place. Sew lace in place. Cut away excess linen at back of lace, allowing for very narrow hem. Hem neatly.

CHAIR SET

Materials: Use one of the following threads in size 30:

CLARK'S O.N.T. MERCERIZED CROCHET, 5 balls of White or Ecru, or 6 balls of any color.

J. & P. COATS MERCERIZED CROCHET, 4 balls of White or Ecru, or 5 balls of any color.

Completed chair back measures about 9½ x 13 inches; arm pieces measure about 7½ x 9½ inches.

CHAIR BACK . . . Motif. Make a four-leaf clover, using shuttle only. R of 4 ds, 3 p's sep. by 4 ds, 4 ds, cl. Join 1st p of each r to last p of adjacent r and join last p of last r to 1st p of 1st r. Tie and cut. Tie shuttle and ball threads. * R of 4 ds, 3 p's sep. by 4 ds, 4 ds, cl. Rw, ch of 4 ds, p, 4 ds, rw. R of 4 ds, join to p of 1st r, 4 ds, 2 p's sep. by 4 ds, 4 ds, cl. Rw, ch of 4 ds, rw. R of 4 ds, 3 p's sep. by 4 ds, 4 ds, cl. Rw, ch of 4 ds, rw. R of 4 ds, 3 p's sep. by 4 ds, 4 ds, cl. Rw, ch of 4 ds, join to p of adjacent ch, 4 ds. Rw, r of 4 ds, join to last p of adjacent r, 4 ds, 2 p's sep. by 4 ds, 4 ds, cl. Rw, ch of 4 ds, p, 4 ds, join to p of center clover, 4 ds, p, 4 ds, rw. Repeat from * 3 more times, joining last ch at base of 1st r. This completes one motif. Make 6 more motifs, joining center p's of corner r's to center p's of corner r's of previous motif (this completes one strip). Make 5 more strips, joining to previous ones by joining center p of corner r's in same place where corner r's were joined previously. Fill in all spaces between motifs as follows: Use shuttle, leaving 15 inches of thread to be used as ball thread, thus avoiding a knot. ** With longest opening of space perpendicularly in front of you, make r of 4 ds, p, 4 ds, join to center p's of the 2 r's at top of opening, 4 ds, p, 4 ds, cl. Rw, ch of 4 ds. Rw, r of 4 ds, join to last p of adjacent r at side of opening, 4 ds, p, 4 ds, join to last p of adjacent r at other side of opening, 4 ds, cl. Rw, ch of 4 ds. Repeat from ** once more, joining last ch at base of 1st r.

ARM PIECES . . . Make 4 x 5 motifs for each arm piece, completing them as for chair back.

CENTER PIECE

MATERIALS REQUIRED: 10 Balls of The American Thread Company's "SILKINE" Crochet Cotton, Article 30, Size 60, White.

Round Medallion:

1st Row: R 8 p separated by 1 d, close r and break thread.

2nd Row: R 3 d, p, 3 d, join to center r, 3 d, p, 3 d, close r. * Ch 2 d, 3 p separated by 1 d, 1 d. R 1 d, 7 p separated by 1 d, 1 d, close r. Ch 2 d, 3 p, separated by 1 d, 2 d. R 3 d, join to last picot of last r, 3 d, join to next picot of center r, 3 d, p, 3 d, close r and repeat from * all around.

3rd Row: Join to second picot of ch, ch 2 d, 5 p, separated by 1 d, 2 d, R 5 d p, p 5 d, close r. Ch 1 d, 5 p separated by 1 d, 2 d, join to second last picot of ch of previous row. Ch 3 d and repeat from beginning.

Square Medallion:

1st Row: R 5 d, p, 5 d, close r and turn work. R 1 d, 5 p separated by 1 d, 1 d, join to small r of round motif, 1 d, 5 p separated by 1 d, 1 d, close r and turn work. Ch 7 d, p, 7 d, turn work. R 5 d, p, 5 d, 5 p separated by 1 d, 1 d, close r. Ch 1 d, p, 1 d. R 4 d, join to seventh picot of first large r, 4 d, close r. Ch 1 d, p, 2 d, turn work. R 4 d, join to last p ot large r, 4 d, close r and turn work. Ch 1 d, 3 p, separated by 1 d, 2 d and turn work. Ch

1 d, p, 1 d. R 4 d, join to next small r of round motif, 4 d, close r. Ch 1 d, p, 2 d, turn work. R 4 d, join to picot of large r, 4 d, close r and turn work. Ch 1 d, 3 p separated by 1 d, 2 d, turn work. R 4 d, join to next picot of large r, 4 d, close r and turn work. Ch 4 d, p, 2 d. R 4 d, p, 4 d, close r. Ch 1 d, p, 1 d, turn work and join to next picot of large r, 7 d, join to picot of first ch, 7 d and repeat from beginning. Work as many motifs as required, arranging them as illustrated.

Border:

1st Row: R 1 d, p, 1 d, join to three small rings where square and round motifs join, 1 d, p, 1 d, close r. * Ch 3 d, p, 3 d. R 1 d, join to last picot of small r, 1 d, p, 1 d, p, 1 d, close r. Ch 3 d, p, 3 d. R 1 d, join to picot of last r, 1 d, p, 1 d, p, 1 d, close r. Ch 3 d, p, 3 d. R 1 d, join to last r, 1 d, p, 1 d, p, 1 d, close r. Ch 3 d, p, 3 d. R 1 d, join to last r, 1 d, join to first free ring of round motif, 1 d, p, 1 d, close r and repeat from * till all free rings have joined and repeat from the beginning.

2nd Row: Join picots of ch on each side of first small r, * Ch 5 d, p, 5 d, join to picot of next ch, repeat from * around scallop and repeat from beginning.

3rd Row: Finish edge with Ch 1 d, 3 p separated by 1 d, 1 d and join to next ch of previous row. At top of scallop join three ch of previous row together as illustrated.

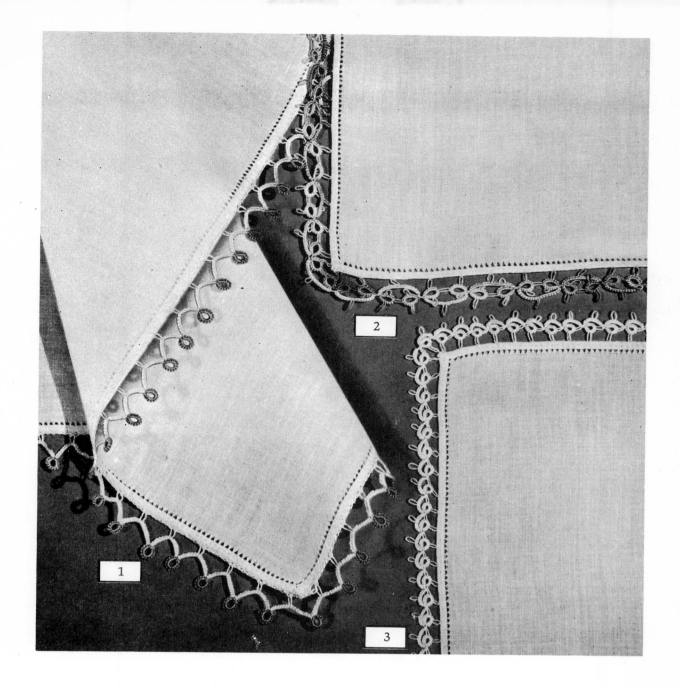

HANDKERCHIEF EDGINGS

Use: J. & P. Coats Tatting Cotton, Clark's O.N.T. or J. & P. Coats Mercerized Crochet

No. 1

Two-color edging.

Use Milward's steel crochet hook. Use shuttle wound with contrasting color, and a ball of White. Tie thread ends of shuttle and ball together. * R of 10 ds, cl. Rw and on ball thread make ch of 5 ds, p, 5 ds. Rw. Repeat from * for length desired. With crochet hook make s c in each p of ch, making ch sts between p's as necessary.

No. 2

Use one shuttle and a ball of thread. Tie thread ends of shuttle and ball. * R of 4 ds, 3 p's sep. by 4 ds, 4 ds, cl. Rw, and on ball thread make ch of 8 ds, p, 8 ds. Rw, r of 4 ds, p, 4 ds, join to center p of first r, 4 ds, p, 4 ds, cl. Rw and repeat from * for length desired.

No. 3

Use one shuttle and a ball of thread. Tie thread ends of shuttle and ball together. * R of 3 ds, p, 3 ds, p, 5 ds, cl. Rw and make ch of 5 ds, p, 5 ds, rw. Join to 2nd p of r. Repeat from * for length desired.

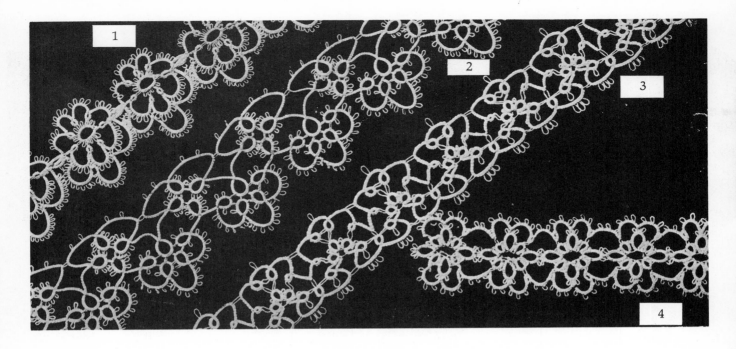

EDGINGS FOR FINE LINENS

No. 2   Tie shuttle and ball threads. **1st row:** R of 3 ds, 8 p's sep. by 3 ds, 3 ds, cl. Rw, ch of 10 ds, 3 p's sep. by 7 ds, 7 ds, rw. * R of 3 ds, 3 p's sep. by 3 ds, 3 ds, join to 5th p of last r, 3 ds, 4 p's sep. by 3 ds, 3 ds, cl. Rw, ch of 7 ds, 3 p's sep. by 7 ds, 10 ds, rw. Make another r like one just made, rw. Ch of 12 ds, rw. Lr of 10 ds, 4 p's sep. by 4 ds, 10 ds, cl. Rw, ch of 12 ds, rw. R of 3 ds, 8 p's sep. by 3 ds, 3 ds, cl. Rw, ch of 10 ds, join to 3rd p made on adjacent ch, 7 ds, p, 7 ds, p, 7 ds, rw. Repeat from * for desired length. **2nd row:** * R of 3 ds, 3 p's sep. by 3 ds, 3 ds, join to 4th p of 1st r of a group of 3 r's, 3 ds, join to nearest p of 3rd r of the group, 3 ds, 3 p's sep. by 3 ds, 3 ds, cl. Rw, ch of 6 ds, rw. R of 4 ds, p, 4 ds, p, 4 ds, join to 1st p of lr, 4 ds, p, 4 ds, p, 4 ds, cl. Rw, ch of 3 ds, 6 p's sep. by 3 ds, 3 ds, rw. R of 4 ds, p, 4 ds, skip 1 p of last r, join to next p of same r, 4 ds, join to next p of lr, 4 ds, p, 4 ds, p, 4 ds, cl. Rw, ch of 3 ds, 8 p's sep. by 3 ds, 3 ds, rw. Make another r like one just made, rw. Ch of 3 ds. 6 p's sep. by 3 ds, 3 ds, rw. Make another r like one just made, rw. Ch of 6 ds, rw. Repeat from * across.

No. 4   **1st row:** Sr of 5 ds, 3 p's sep. by 2 ds, 5 ds, cl. * Lr of 5 ds, join to last p of last r, 5 ds, 4 p's sep. by 1 ds, 5 ds, p, 5 ds, cl. Sr of 5 ds, join to last p of last r, 2 ds, 2 p's sep. by 2 ds, 5 ds, cl. Repeat from * until 4 sr's and 4 lr's are made, joining last p of last r to 1st p of 1st r. Tie and cut. Continue motifs, joining center 2 p's of lr to center 2 p's of·lr on previous motif. **2nd row:** Tie shuttle and ball threads to

center p of 1 sr, make ch of 3 ds, 4 p's sep. by 3 ds, 3 ds, join to 2 center p's of lr, * ch of 3 ds, 4 p's sep. by 3 ds, 3 ds, join to center p of next sr. Ch of 3 ds, join to last p of last ch, 3 ds, 3 p's sep. by 3 ds, 3 ds, join to center p of next sr. Ch of 3 ds, join to last p of last ch, 3 ds, 3 p's sep. by 3 ds, 3 ds, join to 2 center p's of next lr. Repeat from * across. Work opposite side the same.

No. 1   Lr of 2 ds, 14 p's sep. by 2 ds. cl. Tie ends and cut. Tie shuttle and ball threads. Sr of 4 ds, join to p of lr, 4 ds, cl. * Rw, ch of 4 ds, 4 p's sep. by 2 ds, 4 ds, rw. Sr of 4 ds, skip 1 p of lr, join to next p, 4 ds, cl. Repeat from * until 5 sr's are made. ** Rw, ch of 4 ds, 6 p's sep. by 2 ds, 4 ds, rw. Sr of 4 ds, skip 1 p of lr, join to next p, 4 ds, cl. Repeat from ** once more. Rw, ch of 4 ds, 6 p's sep. by 2 ds, 4 ds, join to 1st small r. Tie ends and cut. Lr of 2 ds, 14 p's sep. by 2 ds, cl. Tie and cut. Tie threads. Sr of 4 ds, join to p of lr, 4 ds, cl. *** Rw, ch of 4 ds, 4 p's sep. by 2 ds, 4 ds, rw. Sr of 4 ds, skip 1 p of lr, join to next p, 4 ds, cl. Repeat from *** until 4 ch's and 4 sr's are made. Continuing on ch, make 7 ds, join to loop made by ch of 4 ds and 4 p's (next to ch of 6 p's of 1st flower), 7 ds on same ch, join to beginning of ch of 7 ds. Sr of 4 ds, skip 1 p, join to next p, 4 ds, cl. Complete as for 1st flower. Work thus for desired length. Tie threads to sr next to 6-p ch at outer edge of 1st flower. Ch of 6 ds, 9 p's sep. by 2 ds, 6 ds, join to last p of 1st ch and 1st p of 2nd ch. Ch of 6 ds, 11 p's sep. by 2 ds, 6 ds, join to last p of ch and 1st p of next ch; ch of 6 ds, 9 p's

sep. by 2 ds, 6 ds, join to ch where ch of 7 ds was joined (between motifs). Ch of 4 ds, p, 4 ds, join to corresponding ch on next motif, and continue thus across.

No. 3   Tie shuttle and ball threads. **1st row:** R of 6 ds, 3 p's sep. by 1 ds, 6 ds, cl. * Rw, ch of 4 ds, 3 p's sep. by 2 ds, 4 ds, p, 6 ds, rw. R of 4 ds, p, 4 ds, join to last p of previous r, 4 ds, p, 4 ds, cl. Rw, ch of 4 ds, rw. R of 4 ds, join to last p of previous r, 4 ds, 2 p's sep. by 4 ds, 4 ds, cl. R of 4 ds, join to last p of last r, 4 ds, 2 p's sep. by 2 ds, 4 ds, p, 4 ds, cl. R of 4 ds, join to last p of previous r, 4 ds, p, 4 ds, p, 4 ds, cl (the last 3 r's form clover). Rw, ch of 6 ds. Rw, r of 6 ds, join to p of last r, 4 ds, 2 p's sep. by 4 ds, 4 ds, cl. Rw, ch of 6 ds, join to p of last ch, 4 ds, 3 p's sep. by 2 ds, 4 ds, rw. R of 6 ds, join to center p of previous r, 1 ds, 2 p's sep. by 1 ds, 6 ds, cl. Repeat from * for desired length, ending to correspond with beginning. Tie ends and cut. **2nd row:** Tie threads to center p of last r made. Make ch of 10 ds, rw. R of 4 ds, join to center p of 1st r of clover, 4 ds, cl. Rw, ch of 7 ds, p, 7 ds, rw. * R of 8 ds, join to p of next r, 2 ds, p, 6 ds, cl. Rw, ch of 6 ds, p, 6 ds, rw. R of 6 ds, join to p of last r, 2 ds, join to next p of center r of clover, 8 ds, cl. Rw, ch of 8 ds, p, 6 ds, rw. Sr of 4 ds, join to next p of next r of clover, 4 ds, cl. Rw, ch of 6 ds, join to center p of r between clovers, 6 ds, rw. Sr of 4 ds, join to p of 1st r of next clover, 4 ds, cl. Rw, ch of 6 ds, join to p of last ch, 8 ds, rw. Repeat from * across. Tie ends and cut.

20

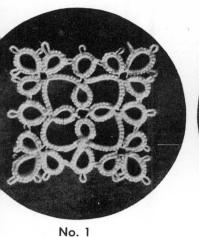

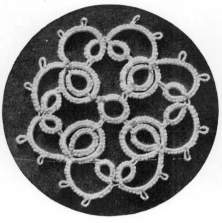

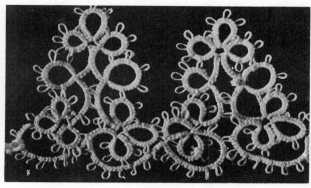

No. 1

No. 2

No. 3

MEDALLIONS & EDGINGS

No. 1

Materials: J. & P. Coats Tatting Cotton, and shuttle.

When completed motif is about 1¼ inches square.

Lr of 6 ds, p, 5 ds, p, 5 ds, p, 6 ds, cl. Rw. Make a center r of 8 ds, p, 8 ds, cl. Rw. * Make a ch of 8 ds. Sr of 5 ds, join to side p of adjacent r, 5 ds, p, 5 ds, cl. Lr of 6 ds, p, 5 ds, p, 5 ds, p, 6 ds, cl. Sr of 3 p's sep. by 5 ds, cl. Ch of 8 ds, rw. R of 8 ds, join to p of center r, 8 ds, cl. Rw. Lr of 6 ds, join to side p of adjacent r, 5 ds, p, 5 ds, p, 6 ds, cl. Repeat from * until 4 center r's are made, then join last sr to 1st lr at the side p. Break off.

No. 2

Materials: Clark's O.N.T. or J. & P. Coats Mercerized Crochet, size 30, 1 ball, and a shuttle.

When completed, medallion measures about 2 inches in diameter.

Starting at center, with shuttle thread make r of 6 ds, 4 p's sep. by 7 ds, 1 ds, cl. Tie securely. Break off. Make lr of 12 ds, join to 1st p of center r, 12 ds, cl. With ball thread make ch of 7 ds, p, 11 ds, join to p of center r where previous r was joined; 11 ds, p, 7 ds, cl by drawing ball thread tightly through tip of ch just made (thus forming double r). Rw. * Continuing with ball thread, make ch of 7 ds, p, 7 ds, p, 7 ds. With shuttle thread make sr of 8 ds, join to p of double r, 8 ds, cl. Make another sr of 8 ds, p, 8 ds, cl. Rw. With ball thread make a ch of 7 ds, p, 7 ds, p, 7 ds. Rw. With shuttle thread make lr of 12 ds, join to next p of center r, 12 ds, cl. Rw. With ball thread make ch of 7 ds, join to p of last sr, 11 ds, join to p of center r where previous r was joined, 11 ds, p, 7 ds, cl as before at tip of ch (thus forming double r). Repeat from *

around, but join last sr to double r, and last ch to tip of double r as before.

No. 3

Use one shuttle and a ball of thread.

Make a ch of 3 ds, 9 p's sep. by 3 ds, 3 ds, rw. With shuttle thread, r of 3 ds, 5 p's sep. by 3 ds, 3 ds, cl. R of 4 ds, join to 1st p of previous r, 4 ds, 4 p's sep. by 4 ds, 4 ds, cl. * R of 3 ds, join to 1st p of previous r, 3 ds, 4 p's sep. by 3 ds, 3 ds, cl. Rw. Make a ch of 4 ds, 4 p's sep. by 4 ds, 4 ds, rw. With shuttle thread, lr of 5 ds, join to 1st p of previous r, 4 ds, 4 p's sep. by 4 ds, 5 ds, cl. Rw. Make a ch of 7 ds, rw. With shuttle thread, r of 3 ds, join to 1st p of lr, 3 ds, 4 p's sep. by 3 ds, 3 ds, cl. R of 4 ds, join to 1st p of previous r, 4 ds, 4 p's sep. by 4 ds, 4 ds, cl. R of 3 ds, join to 1st p of previous r, 3 ds, 4 p's sep. by 3 ds, 3 ds, cl. Rw. Make a ch of 7 ds, rw. With shuttle thread, lr of 5 ds, join to 1st p of previous r, 4 ds, 4 p's sep. by 4 ds, 5 ds, cl. Rw. Make a ch of 4 ds, p, 3 ds, join to 2nd p of adjacent ch, 3 ds, 2 p's sep. by 3 ds, 4 ds, rw. With shuttle thread, r of 3 ds, p, 3 ds, p, 3 ds, join to 1st p of lr, 3 ds, p, 3 ds, p, 3 ds, cl. R of 4 ds, join to 1st p of previous r, 4 ds, 4 p's sep. by 4 ds, 4 ds, cl. R of 3 ds, join to 1st p of previous r, 3 ds, 4 p's sep. by 3 ds, 3 ds, cl. Rw. Make a ch of 3 ds, join to 1st p of previous ch, 3 ds, p, 3 ds, join to 2nd p of 1st ch made, 3 ds, 6 p's sep. by 3 ds, 3 ds. Join to 2nd p of 2nd last r made. Make a ch of 3 ds, join to 1st p of previous ch, 3 ds, 8 p's sep. by 3 ds, 3 ds, rw. With shuttle thread, r of 3 ds, 5 p's sep. by 3 ds, cl. R of 4 ds, join to 1st p of previous r, 3 ds, p, 3 ds, join in same p where previous ch was joined, 3 ds, p, 3 ds, p, 4 ds, cl. Repeat from * for length desired.

DELICATE EDGINGS

No. 1   EDGING . . . Use one shuttle. R of 6 ds, 2 p's sep. by 6 ds, 6 ds, cl, leaving a sp of ⅛ inch at base of r. * R of 6 ds, join to last p of last r, 6 ds, p, 6 ds, cl, leaving a sp as before at base of r. Repeat from * for desired length.

CORNER MOTIF . . . Use one shuttle. **Flower:** * R of 14 ds, cl. Repeat from * 3 more times. Tie ends and cut, Make 6 flowers in all. **Leaves:** R of 4 ds, p, 4 ds, cl. Make another r like this. Tie ends and cut, leaving thread long enough for stems to extend beyond both leaves. Make 5 pairs of leaves. Sew leaves and stems in place through p's and knots. Sew on flowers with yellow sewing thread (yellow forms flower centers).

No. 3   Tie shuttle and ball threads. ** With shuttle make r of 4 ds, 7 p's sep. by 2 ds, 4 ds, cl. * R of 4 ds, join to last p of previous r, 2 ds, 6 p's sep. by 2 ds, 4 ds, cl. Repeat from * 2 more times, joining the last r at both sides. Tie ends securely and cut (a flower made). Repeat from ** for desired length, joining center p of one r to center p of one r of previous flower.

EDGING . . . Attach threads to 1st free p of r opposite joining of flowers, and * make a ch of 6 ds, 7 p's sep. by 2 ds, 6 ds, skip r, join to next p of next r, ch of 3 ds, 2 p's sep. by 2 ds, 3 ds, join to next p of next r. Repeat from * across. Tie ends and cut.

No. 4   Use one shuttle. Make lr of 4 ds, 2 p's sep. by 2 ds, 3 ds, 3 p's sep. by 2 ds, 3 ds, 2 p's sep. by 2 ds, 4 ds, cl. * Sp (¼-inch), sr of 6 ds, join to p of lr, 4 ds, p, 6 ds, cl. Sp, lr of 4 ds, join to p of sr, 2 ds, join to p of lr, 3 ds, 3 p's sep. by 2 ds, 3 ds, 2 p's sep. by 2 ds, 4 ds, cl. Repeat from * for desired length.

No. 2   Use one shuttle. Make lr of 4 ds, 3 p's sep. by 4 ds, 4 ds, cl. * Rw, sp (¼-inch), make a Josephine knot of 10 single sts, rw. Sp, lr of 4 ds, join to p of last lr, 4 ds, p, 4 ds, p, 4 ds, cl. Repeat from * for desired length.

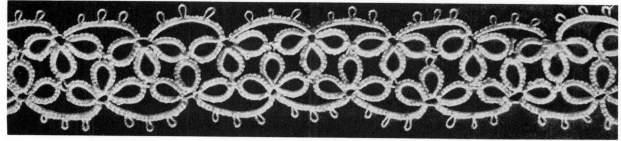

No. 1

No. 2

No. 3

No. 4

EDGINGS FOR ALL OCCASIONS

No. 1

Use one shuttle and a ball of thread.

R of 10 ds, p, 10 ds, cl. Make 2 more r's same as this. * Rw, make a ch of 3 p's sep. by 5 ds, rw. R of 10 ds, join to p of adjacent r, 10 ds, cl. Make 2 more r's, but without joining to any p's. Repeat from * across for length desired. Break off. This is one half of insertion. Work other half as follows: R of 10 ds, p, 10 ds, cl. ** R of 10 ds, join to joining of 2 p's of first half of insertion, 10 ds, cl. R of 10 ds, join to free p of center r of group on first half of insertion, 10 ds, cl. Rw. Make a ch of 3 p's sep. by 5 ds, rw. R of 10 ds, join to joining of 2 r's just made, 10 ds, cl. Repeat from ** across. Break off.

No. 2

Use one shuttle and a ball of thread.

With shuttle thread make r of 4 ds, p, 3 more p's sep. by 3 ds, 4 ds, cl. * Rw, attach ball thread, 7 ds, p, 5 ds, p, 7 ds, rw. With shuttle thread r of 4 ds, p, 3 ds, join to 2nd p of 1st r, 3 ds, p, 3 ds, p, 4 ds, cl. R of 4 ds, p, 3 more p's sep. by 3 ds, 4 ds, cl. Repeat from * for length desired (this completes first half of insertion). Work other half to correspond, but join the p's on ch to the p's on ch of previous half while working.

No. 3

Center r. 8 p's sep. by 3 ds, cl. Break off. R of 5 ds, p, 4 ds, p, 2 ds, p, 4 ds, p, 5 ds, cl. Sp

(⅛-inch), join to a p of center r, * sp (⅛-inch), r of 5 ds, join to p of adjacent r, 4 ds, p, 2 ds, p, 4 ds, p, 5 ds, cl. Sp (⅛-inch), join to next p of center r. Repeat from * around (8 rings in all). Join and break off. Make another wheel same as this, but join one r at the 2 p's to 1st wheel and complete round. Break off. Continue in this manner for length desired.

No. 4

Use one shuttle and a ball of thread. Tie shuttle and ball threads together. R of 4 ds, lp, 4 ds, cl. Rw, ch of 3 ds, 4 lp's sep. by 2 ds, 3 ds. Rw, r of 4 ds, join to lp of 1st r made, 4 ds, cl. R of 4 ds, lp, 4 ds, cl. Rw, ch of 3 ds, 4 lp's sep. by 2 ds, 3 ds. * Rw, r of 4 ds, join to lp of last r made, 4 ds, cl. Rw, ch of 3 ds, 4 lp's sep. by 2 ds, 3 ds. Rw, r of 4 ds, join to same lp to which last r is joined, 4 ds, cl. Rw, ch of 3 ds, 4 lp's sep. by 2 ds, 3 ds. Rw, r of 4 ds, join to last lp, 4 ds, cl. R of 4 ds, join to 1st lp, 4 ds, cl. Rw, ch of 3 ds, 4 lp's sep. by 2 ds, 3 ds. Rw, r of 4 ds, join to 1st lp, 4 ds, cl. Rw, ch of 4 ds, lp, 2 ds, lp, 4 ds. Rw, r of 4 ds, lp, 4 ds. Rw, ch of 3 ds, lp, 2 ds, sk 1st lp of adjacent ch, join to next lp, 2 ds, join to next lp of same ch, 2 ds, lp, 3 ds. Rw, r of 4 ds, join to lp of sr, 4 ds, cl. R of 4 ds, lp, 4 ds, cl. Rw, ch of 3 ds, lp, 2 ds, sk 1 lp of adjacent ch, join to next lp, 2 ds, join to next lp of same ch, 2 ds, lp, 3 ds. Repeat from * for length desired.

TRAY MAT

Materials: CLARK'S O.N.T. or J. & P. COATS MERCERIZED CROCHET, size 30, 2 balls of White, Ecru or any color.

Completed mat measures about 11 x 19 inches.

MOTIF . . . **1st rnd:** Tie shuttle and ball threads. Lr of 5 ds, p, 5 ds, 3 p's sep. by 3 ds, 5 ds, p, 5 ds, cl. Rw, ch of 5 ds, 3 p's sep. by 5 ds, 5 ds. Rw, lr of 5 ds, join to last p of previous r, 5 ds, 3 p's sep. by 3 ds, 5 ds, p, 5 ds, cl. Rw, ch like 1st ch. Rw, lr of 5 ds, join to last p of previous r, 5 ds, 3 p's sep. by 3 ds, 5 ds, p, 5 ds, cl. Rw, ch like last ch (all ch's in this rnd are the same). Rw, lr like 1st r, joining 3rd p to 3rd p of last r and complete r. Rw, sr of 5 ds, 3 p's sep. by 4 ds, 5 ds, cl. Make another sr like this. Ch as before. Rw, lr like 1st lr, joining 3rd p where last lr was joined. Rw, ch as before. Rw, lr of 5 ds, join to last p of last lr, 5 ds, p, 3 ds, join to center p of adjacent lr, 3 ds, p, 5 ds, p, 5 ds, cl. Rw, ch as before. Rw, lr, join to last p of last lr, 5 ds, p, 3 ds, join to center p of adjacent r, 3 ds, p, 5 ds, p, 5 ds, cl. Rw, ch. Rw, lr, joining 3rd p where last lr was joined, and complete r. Rw, make 2 sr's as before. Ch as before, join to base of 1st lr. Tie and cut threads. **2nd rnd:** Tie threads. R of 4 ds, p, 4 ds, p, 4 ds, join to 3rd p of ch made after 2 sr's on 1st rnd; 4 ds, p, 4 ds, p, 4 ds, cl. Rw, ch of 6 ds, p, 5 ds, p, 5 ds, p, 6 ds. Rw and repeat r's and ch's around motif, joining center p of 1 r to center p of each ch and to 2nd p of each r (12 r's and 12 ch's). Join last ch to base of 1st lr. Make 15 more motifs

(Continued on page 26.)

TATTING FOR YOUR HOME

CHAIR SET

Materials: CLARK'S O.N.T. or J. & P. COATS MERCERIZED CROCHET, size 30, 3 balls of White, Ecru, or any color.

ARM PIECES. **Motif** . . . Tie shuttle and ball threads. Lr of 12 ds, lp, 12 ds, cl. Rw, ch of 7 ds, p, 7 ds, p, 7 ds. Rw, lr of 12 ds, join to lp of 1st r, 12 ds, cl. Rw, ch like 1st ch. Rw, lr joined to same lp. Rw, sr of 5 ds, lp, 5 ds, cl. Rw, ch of 5 ds, p, 5 ds. Rw, sr of 5 ds, join to lp of 1st sr, 5 ds, cl. Rw, ch of 10 ds, lp, 10 ds. Rw, sr of 5 ds, join to same lp of sr-group, 5 ds, cl. Rw, ch of 5 ds, p, 5 ds, rw, sr as before, joined to same lp. Rw, ** lr of 12 ds, lp, 12 ds, cl. Rw, ch of 7 ds, join to adjacent p of ch, 7 ds, p, 7 ds. Rw, make lr, joining to last lp. Rw, ch as before. Rw, lr, joined to same lp. Rw, ch as before. Rw, lr joined to same lp. Rw, sr like 1st sr, rw, ch of 5 ds, join to adjacent p of ch, 5 ds. Rw, sr, joined to last sr. Rw, ch of 10 ds, join to lp at center of ch, 10 ds. Rw, sr joined to 1st sr. Rw, ch 5 ds, p, 5 ds. Rw, sr, join to same lp. Repeat from

(Continued on page 26.)

REFRESHMENT SET

Materials: CLARK'S O.N.T. or J. & P. COATS MERCERIZED CROCHET, size 30, 3 balls of White, Ecru, or any color.

Completed centerpiece measures about 14 inches in diameter (measuring at longest points). Each glass doily measures 5½ inches in diameter.

GLASS DOILY . . . Tie shuttle and ball threads. Sr of 8 ds, p, 8 ds, cl. Rw, ch of 6 ds, p, 8 ds, p, 8 ds, p, 6 ds. Rw, sr of 4 ds, p, 4 ds, join to p of 1st sr, 4 ds, p, 4 ds, cl. Lr of 4 ds, join to last p of sr, 8 ds, p, 8 ds, p, 4 ds, cl. * Sr of 4 ds, join to last p of lr, 4 ds, p, 4 ds, p, 4 ds, cl (clover). Rw, ch of 6 ds, join to p of adjacent ch, 8 ds, p, 8 ds, p, 6 ds. Rw, sr of 8 ds, join to center p of last sr, 8 ds, cl. Rw, ch of 6 ds, p, 8 ds, p, 8 ds, p, 6 ds. Rw, sr of 4 ds, p, 4 ds, join to p where last sr was joined, 4 ds, p, 4 ds, cl. Lr of 4 ds, join to last p of sr, 8 ds, join to center p of lr, 8 ds, p, 4 ds, cl. Repeat from * until 3 clovers are made. Rw, ch of 6 ds, join to p of

adjacent ch, 8 ds, p, 8 ds, p, 6 ds. Rw, sr of 8 ds, join to center p of sr, 8 ds, cl. Rw, ch of 8 ds, p, 8 ds. Rw, r of 10 ds, lp (¼-inch), 10 ds, cl. (This begins center of medallion). Rw, ch of 8 ds, join to p of last ch, 8 ds. Rw, sr of 8 ds, p, 8 ds, cl. Rw, ch of 6 ds, join to p of adjacent ch (in 1st section of medallion), 8 ds, join to next p of same ch, 8 ds, p, 6 ds. ** Rw, sr of 4 ds, p, 4 ds, join to p of last sr, 4 ds, p, 4 ds, cl. Lr of 4 ds, join to last p of sr, 8 ds, p, 8 ds, p, 4 ds, cl. Sr of 4 ds, join to last p, 4 ds, p, 4 ds, p, 4 ds, cl. Rw, ch of 6 ds, join to p of adjacent ch, 8 ds, join to p of next ch, 8 ds, join to next p of same ch, 6 ds. Rw, sr of 8 ds, join to center p of sr, 8 ds, cl. Rw, ch of 6 ds, p, 8 ds, p, 8 ds, p, 6 ds. Repeat from ** until 4 clovers are made. Rw, ch of 6 ds, join to p of adjacent ch, 8 ds, p, 8 ds, p, 6 ds. Rw, sr of 8 ds, join where 3 sr's are joined, 8 ds, cl. Rw, ch of 8 ds, p, 8 ds, rw. R of 10 ds, join to p of center, 10 ds, cl. Ch of 8 ds, join to p of adjacent ch, 8 ds. Continue as before until 6

(Continued on page 26.)

OCCASIONAL DOILY

Materials: CLARK'S O.N.T. or J. & P. COATS MERCERIZED CROCHET, size 20, 1 ball of White or Ecru.

Completed doily measures about 7 inches in diameter.

CENTER MOTIF . . . **1st rnd:** Make 4 r's of 8 ds, p, 8 ds, cl. Tie ends but do not cut. **2nd rnd:** (Back of motif) R of 4 ds, 5 p's sep. by 3 ds, 4 ds, cl. Make 5 more r's like this, joining each by 1st p to last p of preceding r. Join last r to 1st p of 1st r. Tie ends and cut. **3rd rnd:** Tie shuttle and ball threads to center p of r on back of motif; * ch of 5 ds, 2 p's sep. by 5 ds, 5 ds, join to center p of next r. Repeat from * around. Join to p where rnd began. Do not cut threads. **4th rnd:** * Ch of 5 ds, 5 p's sep. by 4 ds, 5 ds, join to next joining on 3rd rnd. Repeat from * 5 more times. Join to p where row began. Tie ends and cut. Make 6 more motifs like this, joining to center one as follows: When making 4th ch of 2nd motif, join by 4th p to 4th p of 1st motif. Make next ch as far as 2nd p; join to 2nd p of next ch of 1st motif. Finish as before. The 3rd and all other motifs are joined first by 3rd p of ch to 3rd p of 1st free ch above joining of preceding motif; then to center motif as 2nd motif was joined. The 7th motif will be joined by both side ch's to 2nd and 6th motifs. **Next rnd:** Join threads to joining of 2 motifs. * Ch of 4 ds, 5 p's sep. by 4 ds, 4 ds. Join to center p of next ch. Repeat from * once more. Ch of 4 ds, 5 p's sep. by 4 ds, 4 ds, join to p where 2 motifs are joined. Continue thus around.

Chair Set
(Continued from page 25.)

** until 6 ch's are joined at center and 6 groups of lr's are completed; but,

when making last group of sr's, finish as follows: Make and join 3rd sr, make ch of 5 ds, join to p of opposite ch (of 1st group), 5 ds. Make sr, join as before. Make lr, join to 1st group of lr's. Finish group with a ch, join to base of 1st lr. Tie ends and cut.

To Join Motifs: Work 2nd motif until 2 groups of lr's are made. Make 2 r's in next group, make a ch of 7 ds, p, 7 ds, join to corresponding p of 1st motif, 7 ds. Rw, lr, join to lp, rw, ch of 7 ds, join to p of next ch on 1st motif, 7 ds, p, 7 ds. Rw, make 4th lr, joining to same group. Make group of sr's, joined to center p, work 1st lr of next group. Rw, ch of 7 ds, join to p of last ch, 7 ds, join to p of next ch of 1st motif, 7 ds. Rw, make 2nd lr. Rw, ch of 7 ds, join to p of next ch on 1st motif. This completes the joining of 2 motifs. When joining where 2 motifs are already joined, continue corner ch of 7 ds, join to 1st free p of next motif. Continue thus, joining next 3 p's to corner.

CHAIR BACK . . . Join 5 motifs for 1st row, 4 motifs for 2nd row, 3 motifs for 3rd row, 2 motifs for 4th row, and 1 motif for 5th row.

Tray Mat
(Continued from page 24.)

like this, joining center p of 3rd ch of 2nd rnd to 3rd p of adjacent ch of 1st motif and complete rnd. Join 6 motifs like this for center row of mat. There are 5 motifs in each side row, joined as follows: 1st motif of side row is worked until 4 r's and 3 ch's are made; 4th ch is worked 6 ds, p, 5 ds, join 1st p, to 1st ch of 1st motif of center row, 5 ds, join to next p of 1st motif, 6 ds. Make another r, ch as before, another r, and ch of 6 ds, skip 1 ch of 2nd motif of center row, join to 2nd p of next ch, 5 ds, join to next p, 5 ds, p, 6 ds, and

complete rnd. To join next motif, when making 2nd ch make 6 ds, p, 5 ds, join to center p of adjacent side of ch of 1st motif on second row. Make 1 unjoined ch. When making next ch, make 6 ds, p, 5 ds, skip 1 ch of 2nd motif of center row, join to 1st and 2nd p's of next ch. Make 1 free ch, skip 1 ch of 3rd motif of center row, join next ch to 2nd and 3rd p's of next ch, and complete rnd. Continue thus until 5 motifs are joined. Make another row like this on opposite side of center row.

TRIANGULAR JOINING BARS . . . Attach threads to 2nd p of free ch, make a ch of 13 ds, join to 2nd p of next free ch. Ch of 13 ds, join to 2nd p of next free ch, ch of 13 ds, join to 1st p. Tie ends and cut.

EDGING . . . **1st rnd:** Join threads to center p of any outside ch. * Ch of 4 ds, lp (⅜-inch), 4 ds, 6 lp's sep. by 4 ds, 4 ds, join to center p of next ch. Repeat from * around. Tie and cut. **2nd rnd:** Attach threads to 5th p of any ch, ** ch of 2 ds, lp, 2 ds, join to last p of same ch and 1st p of next ch. * Ch of 2 ds, p, 2 ds, join to next p. Repeat from * 4 more times. Repeat from ** around.

Refreshment Set
(Continued from page 25.)

sections are made, joining the 6th section to first as others were joined. Now complete 1st section, joining ch's to 6th section. Tie threads securely and cut.

CENTERPIECE . . . Make 7 doilies as for glass doily, joining 2nd doily to 1st by p's on 4 ch's (2 ch's on each of 2 sections). When joining the 3rd doily to 1st and 2nd, join along 2 of its sides (8 ch's in all). The 7th doily will be joined on 3 sides.

DISTINCTIVE LUNCHEON SET

Materials: CLARK'S O.N.T. or J. & P. COATS MERCERIZED CROCHET, size 20, 4 balls of White or Ecru.

PLATE DOILY . . . **1st rnd:** Tie shuttle and ball threads. Make r of 2 ds, 5 p's sep. by 2 ds, 2 ds, cl. Rw, ch of 6 ds, 4 p's sep. by 4 ds, 6 ds. Rw, r of 2 ds, p, 2 ds, skip 1 p of last r, join to next p, 2 ds, p, 2 ds, p, 2 ds, 2 ds, cl. Continue thus until 7 r's and 7 ch's are made. Rw, 2 ds, p, 2 ds, join to adjacent r, 2 ds, p, 2 ds, join to 2nd p of 1st r, 2 ds, p, 2 ds, cl. Rw, ch of 6 ds, 4 p's sep. by 4 ds, 6 ds, join to base of 1st r. Tie ends and cut. **2nd rnd:** R of 3 ds, p, 3 ds, join to 2nd p of ch on 1st rnd, 3 ds, p, 3 ds, cl. Rw, ch of 7 ds, p, 7 ds. Rw, r of 3 ds, p, 3 ds, join to next p of same ch, 3 ds, p, 3 ds, cl. Continue thus until 16 r's and 16 ch's are made. Join and tie securely; cut threads. **3rd rnd:** R of 3 ds, p, 3 ds, join to p of ch on previous rnd, 3 ds, p, 3 ds, cl. * Rw, ch of 5 ds, p, 5 ds, p, 5 ds, p, 5 ds. Rw, r of 3 ds, p, 3 ds, join to p of next ch, 3 ds, p,

3 ds, cl. Repeat from * around. Join last ch to base of 1st r. Tie and cut. **4th rnd:** R of 3 ds, p, 3 ds, join to 1st p of 1st ch on 3rd rnd, 3 ds, p, 3 ds, cl. Rw, sp (⅛-inch). R of 4 ds, 3 p's sep. by 4 ds, 4 ds, cl. Rw, sp. R of 3 ds, join to last p of adjacent r, 3 ds, join to next p of ch, 3 ds, p, 3 ds, cl. Rw, sp. R of 4 ds, join to last p of adjacent r, 4 ds, p, 4 ds, p, 4 ds, cl. Rw, sp. R of 3 ds, join to last p of adjacent r, 3 ds, join to next p of ch, 3 ds, p, 3 ds, cl. Rw, sp. R of 4 ds, join to last p of adjacent r, 4 ds, p, 4 ds, p, 4 ds, cl. Continue thus around, joining last p's of last 2 r's to 1st p's of 1st 2 r's made. Tie and cut. **5th rnd:** Tie shuttle and ball threads. R of 4 ds, p, 4 ds, join to p of previous rnd, 4 ds, p, 4 ds, cl. * Rw, ch of 9 ds, p, 9 ds. Rw, r of 4 ds, p, 4 ds, skip 1 r, join to p of next r, 4 ds, p, 4 ds, cl. Repeat from * around, joining last ch to base of 1st r. Tie and cut. **6th rnd:** R of 4 ds, p, 4 ds, join to p of previous ch, 4 ds, p, 4 ds, cl. Rw, ch of 5 ds, 3 p's sep. by 5 ds, 5 ds. Rw, r of 4 ds, p, 4 ds, join to p of next

ch, 4 ds, p, 4 ds, cl. Continue thus around, joining last ch to base of 1st r. Tie and cut. **7th rnd:** With shuttle make r of 4 ds, p, 4 ds, join to 1st p of ch on previous rnd, 4 ds, p, 4 ds, cl. Rw, sp (⅛-inch). R of 5 ds, 3 p's sep. by 5 ds, 5 ds, cl. Rw, sp. R of 4 ds, join to last p of adjacent r, 4 ds, join to next p of ch, 4 ds, p, 4 ds, cl. Rw, sp. R of 5 ds, join to last p of adjacent r, 5 ds, p, 5 ds, p, 5 ds, cl. Rw, sp. R of 4 ds, join to last p of adjacent r, 4 ds, join to next p of ch, 4 ds, p, 4 ds, cl. Rw, sp. R of 5 ds, join to last p of adjacent r, 5 ds, p, 5 ds, p, 5 ds, cl. Continue thus around, joining last r's as in 4th rnd. Tie and cut. **8th rnd:** Tie shuttle and ball threads. R of 4 ds, p, 4 ds, join to p of previous rnd, 4 ds, p, 4 ds, cl. Rw, ch of 9 ds, p, 9 ds. Rw, r of 4 ds, p, 4 ds, skip 1 r, join to p of next r of previous rnd, 4 ds, p, 4 ds, cl. Continue thus around; join last ch to base of 1st r. Tie and cut. **9th rnd:** Tie threads. R of 4 ds, p, 4 ds, join to p of ch of previous rnd, 4 ds, p, 4 ds, cl. Rw, ch of 5 ds, 3 p's sep. by 5 ds, 5 ds. Rw, r of 4 ds, p, 4 ds, join to p

(Continued on page 29.)

27

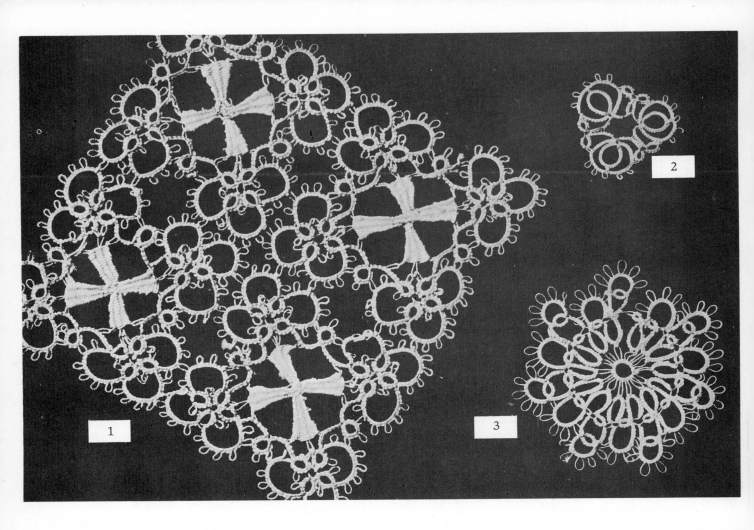

TATTING MOTIFS

No. 1   TABLECLOTH MOTIF.
This motif is particularly suited for a tablecloth or place mats . . . Tie shuttle and ball threads. Sr of 3 ds, 3 p's sep. by 3 ds, 3 ds, cl. * Rw, ch of 4 ds, p, 4 ds. Rw, r of 3 ds, 3 p's sep. by 3 ds, 3 ds, cl. Rw, ch of 3 ds, p, 3 ds, join to p of previous r, 3 ds, 4 p's sep. by 3 ds, 3 ds, rw. R of 3 ds, p, 3 ds, join to center p of last r, 3 ds, p, 3 ds, cl. Rw, ch of 3 ds, 6 p's sep. by 3 ds, 3 ds, rw. R of 3 ds, p, 3 ds, join to p where last r's were joined, 3 ds, p, 3 ds, cl. Rw, ch of 3 ds, 6 p's sep. by 3 ds, 3 ds, rw. R of 3 ds, p, 3 ds, join to p where last r's were joined, 3 ds, p, 3 ds, cl. Rw, ch of 4 ds, p, 4 ds, rw. R of 3 ds, skip 1 p of 6-p ch, join to next p, 3 ds, p, 3 ds, p, 3 ds, cl. Repeat

from * until 4 groups of sr's are made, rw. Ch of 4 ds, p, 4 ds. Join to base of 1st r made. Tie ends and cut.

WEAVING . . . Thread needle and draw through 2 p's of sr's at base of 4-sr group, then draw the needle through the 2 p's of sr's directly opposite, tie 2 ends securely at center (thus forming a bar). Make another bar like this, but join opposite corners. * Then make a bar from p at center of ch on one side to p at center of ch at opposite side, always fastening at center. Repeat from * until 3 bars are made for each corner. Then weave over only 3 bars at one time, picking up 1 bar, passing over next bar, and picking up last bar; on next row pick up the bar which was

passed over in previous row and pass over the bars which were picked up. Alternate these 2 rows until bar is completely covered. Fasten off. Weave over the remaining bars in same way, thus completing 1 motif.

Make motifs for size of article desired, joining the 5th p of 6-p loop and the 2nd p of next 6-p loop to corresponding p's of previous motif.

No. 2   Tie shuttle and ball threads. R of 5 ds, p, 5 ds, cl. R of 5 ds, p, 5 ds, cl. Rw, ch of 4 ds, p, 4 ds. * Rw, r of 14 ds, p, 14 ds, cl. Ch of 9 ds. Join to p of 2nd sr, 3 ds, 2 p's sep. by 3 ds, 3 ds, join to p of lr, p, 3 ds, 3 p's sep. by 3 ds, 9 ds, join to base of lr.

28

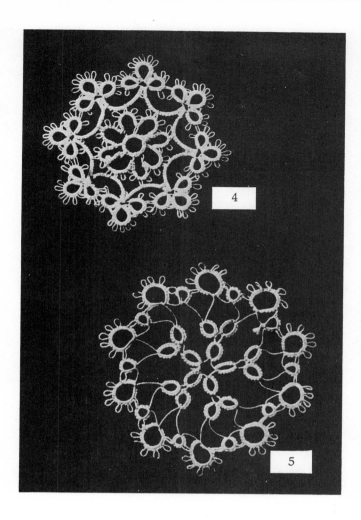

Rw, ch of 4 ds, p, 4 ds, sr of 5 ds, join to last p of outside r, 5 ds, cl. Sr of 5 ds, p, 5 ds, cl. Ch of 4 ds, join to p of last ch, 4 ds. Repeat from * until there are 3 lr's and outside rings, joining last p of last outside ch to p of 1st sr. Ch of 4 ds, join to p of 1st ch, 4 ds, join to base of 1st r. Tie ends and cut.

No. 3 Use a shuttle and a ball of thread. With shuttle make r of 1 ds, 14 p's sep. by 1 ds, cl. Tie ends and cut. Tie shuttle and ball threads. R of 4 ds, p, 4 ds, cl. * Rw, ch of 10 ds, join to p of center r, ch of 10 ds, join to base of previous r, ch of 3 ds, 5 p's sep. by 3 ds, 6 p's, rw. R of 4 ds, join to base of previous r, 4 ds, cl. Rw, ch of 10 ds, join to next p of center r, ch of 10 ds, join to base of previous r, ch of 6 ds, join to p of ch, ch of 3 ds, 5 p's sep. by 3 ds, 3 ds, rw. R of 6 ds, join in same place as ch's were joined, 6 ds, cl. Rw, ch of 6 ds, rw. R of 4 ds, join to base of previous r. Repeat from * around, ending with r of 6 ds, join to same place as ch's were joined, 6 ds, cl. Rw, ch of 6 ds, join to base of 1st r. Tie ends and cut.

No. 4 Use shuttle and a ball of thread. **1st rnd:** With shuttle make 1r of 3 ds, 8 p's sep. by 4 ds, 1 ds, cl. Tie ends securely and cut. **2nd rnd:** Tie shuttle and ball threads to one p-loop, make a ch of 3 ds, 5 p's sep. by 2 ds, 3 ds, * join to next p, ch of 3 ds, join to last p of last ch, 2 ds, 4 p's sep. by 2 ds, 3 ds. Repeat from * around. Join last ch on both ends. Tie ends and cut. **3rd rnd:** Tie threads. With shuttle make r of 5 ds, 5 p's sep. by 2 ds, 5 ds, cl. Lr of 5 ds, join to p of sr, 2 ds, 6 p's sep. by 2 ds, 5 ds, cl. Sr of 5 ds, join to p of lr, 2 ds, 4 p's sep. by 2 ds, 5 ds, cl. Rw and make a ch of 3 ds, p, 7 ds, join to center p of r on 2nd rnd, * 7 ds, p, 3 ds, rw. Sr of 5 ds, p, 2 ds, skip 1 p of previous sr, join to next p, 2 ds, 3 p's sep. by 2 ds, 5 ds, cl. Lr of 5 ds, join to p of sr, 6 p's sep. by 2 ds, 5 ds, cl. Sr of 5 ds, join to p of 1r, 2 ds, 4 p's sep. by 2 ds, 5 ds, cl. Rw and make ch of 3 ds, join to p of last ch, 7 ds, join to center p on next r of 2nd rnd. Repeat from * around, joining 3rd p of last sr to 2nd p of 1st sr, and last ch to p at beginning of 1st ch.

No. 5 **1st rnd:** * R of 8 ds, p, 8 ds, cl. Sp (⅛-inch). Repeat from * 4 more times. Tie ends and cut. **2nd rnd:** Lr of 5 ds, 7 p's sep. by 3 ds, 5 ds, cl. Rw, sp (¼-inch), sr of 8 ds, join to p of 1st rnd, 8 ds, cl. ** Rw, sp (¼-inch), r of 4 ds, join to 1st p of lr, 4 ds, p, 4 ds, cl. Sp, lr of 5 ds, join to p of sr, 3 ds, 6 p's sep. by 3 ds, 5 ds, cl. Rw, sp. Sr of 8 ds, join to same p as last sr was joined in 1st rnd, 8 ds, cl. Rw, sp.

R of 4 ds, join to 1st p of lr, 4 ds, p, 4 ds, cl. Sp, lr of 5 ds, join to p of sr, 3 ds, 6 p's sep. by 3 ds, 5 ds, cl. Rw, sp. Sr of 8 ds, join to next p of 1st rnd, 8 ds, cl. Repeat from ** around, taking care to join the last sr to both lr's to complete rnd.

Distinctive Luncheon Set
(Continued from page 27.)

of next ch, 4 ds, p, 4 ds, cl. Continue thus around, joining last ch to base of 1st r. Tie and cut.

EDGING . . . R of 4 ds, p, 4 ds, join to 1st p of ch of previous rnd, 4 ds, p, 4 ds, cl. * Rw, sp (⅛-inch). R of 5 ds, p, 5 ds, cl. Rw, sp. R of 4 ds, join to last p of adjacent r, 4 ds, join to next p of ch, 4 ds, p, 4 ds, cl. Rw, sp. Lr of 4 ds, join to p of adjacent r, 2 ds, 4 p's sep. by 2 ds, 4 ds, cl. Rw, sp. R of 4 ds, join to last p of adjacent r, 4 ds, join to next p of ch, 4 ds, p, 4 ds, cl. Rw, sp. R of 5 ds, join to last p of previous lr, 5 ds, cl. Rw, sp. R of 4 ds, join to last p of previous r, 4 ds, join to next p of next ch, 4 ds, p, 4 ds, cl. Repeat from * around (36 scallops). Tie and cut.

BREAD AND BUTTER PLATE DOILY . . . Work 6 rnds as for plate doily and finish as before (24 scallops).

GLASS DOILY . . . Work 3 rnds and finish as for plate doily (16 scallops).

EXQUISITE LUNCHEON SET

Materials: Clark's O.N.T. (4 balls) or J. & P. Coats (3 balls) Mercerized Crochet, size 50, White or Ecru. This amount is sufficient for the three doilies.

A shuttle.

The place doily measures about 9¾ inches in diameter, the bread and butter plate doily measures about 8¾ inches in diameter, and the globlet doily measures about 6 inches in diameter.

Place Doily. Starting at center make r of 1 ds, 5 p's sep. by 3 ds, 2 ds, cl. Tie securely and cut off. **1st rnd:** R of 8 ds, join to p of center r, 8 ds, cl. Rw. Attach ball thread. * Make ch of 4 ds, p, 5 ds, p, 4 ds. Rw, r of 8 ds, join to next p of center r, 8 ds, cl, rw. Repeat from * around. Join last ch to 1st r. Tie securely and cut off. **2nd rnd:** R of 8 ds, join to p of ch of previous rnd, 8 ds, cl, rw. Attach ball thread and * ch of 4 ds, p, 5 ds, p, 4 ds. Rw. R of 8 ds, join to next p of ch of previous rnd, 8 ds, cl. Rw. Make ch same as before. Repeat from * around. Join. Tie securely and cut off. **3rd rnd:** R of 8 ds, join to p of ch of previous rnd, 8 ds, cl. Rw. * Ch of 7 ds, p, 7 ds, rw. R of 8 ds, join to next p of ch, 8 ds, cl. Rw. Repeat from * around. Join. Tie securely and cut off. **4th rnd:** R of 8 ds, join to p of ch of previous rnd, 8 ds, cl. Rw. * Ch of 5 ds, p, 6 ds, p, 5 ds. Rw. R of 8 ds, join to next p of ch, 8 ds, cl. Rw. Repeat from * around. Join. Tie securely and cut off. **5th rnd:** R of 8 ds, join to p of ch, 8 ds, cl. Rw. * Ch of 5 ds, p, 5 ds. Rw. R of 8 ds, join to next p, 8 ds, cl. Rw. Repeat from * around. Join. Tie securely and cut off. (40 r's and 40 ch's in rnd.) **6th and 7th rnds:** R of 8 ds, join to p of ch, 8 ds, cl. Rw. * Ch of 8 ds, p, 8 ds. Rw. R of 8 ds, join to next p of ch, 8 ds, cl. Rw. Repeat from * around. Join. Tie securely and cut off. **8th rnd:** R of 8 ds, join to p of ch, 8 ds, cl. Rw. Ch of 5 ds, p, 2 ds, p, 2 ds, p, 5 ds. Rw. Repeat from * around. Join, tie and cut.

Border. R of 4 ds, p, 2 ds, p, 2 ds, p, 4 ds, cl. Rw. Attach ball thread and make a ch of 5 ds, p, 2 ds. Rw. R of 5 ds, join to last p of previous r, 2 ds, p, 3 ds, p, 2 ds, p, 5 ds, cl. Rw. Ch of 5 ds, p, 2 ds. Rw. R of 5 ds, join to last p of previous r, 2 ds, p, 3 ds, p, 2 ds, p, 5 ds, cl. Rw. Ch of 5 ds, p, 2 ds. Rw. R of 5 ds, join to last p of previous r, 2 ds, p, 3 ds, p 2 ds, p, 5 ds, cl. Rw. Ch of 5 ds, p, 2 ds, rw. P, rw, and continue with ch of 6 ds, p, 6 ds. Rw. R of 5 ds, join to reverse p, 3 ds, join to 4th p of previous r, 3 ds, p, 5 ds, cl. Rw. Ch of 2 ds, p, 5 ds. Rw. R of 5 ds, join to 3rd p of previous r, 2 ds, join to 3rd p of adjacent r, 3 ds, join to next p of same r, 2 ds, p, 5 ds, cl. Rw. Ch of 2 ds, p, 5 ds. Rw. * R of 5 ds, join to 4th p of previous r, 2 ds, join to 3rd p of adjacent r, 3 ds, join to next p of same r, 2 ds, p, 5 ds, cl. Rw. Ch of 2 ds, p, 5 ds. Rw. Repeat from * once more. Then, r of 4 ds, join to 4th p of previous r, 2 ds, join to p of adjacent sr, 2 ds, join to next p of same r, 4 ds, cl. Rw. Ch of 4 ds, p, 4 ds, join to 1st p on ch of doily (counting from left), 4 ds, join p where last 2 sr's were joined, 4 ds, join to 1st p of next ch and to the left, 4 ds, p, 4 ds, join to base of 1st sr made. Tie securely and cut threads. Continue in this manner around, joining each point to previous one at 1st p of 1st ch made.

(Continued on next page)

CORNER

DECORATIVE CORNER

Materials: Clark's O.N.T. or J. & P. Coats Mercerized Crochet, size 30, 1 ball, and two shuttles.

When completed, triangle measures about 5½ inches on one straight side.

Tie shuttle threads together. The 4 inner r's of each medallion, and the ch's, including the curved ch which forms the largest outside r's, are made with the 1st shuttle. For all ch's, the 2nd shuttle is used the same as a ball thread. The 2nd shuttle is also used for making the 8 outide r's of each medallion. Inner r of 6 ds, p, 6 ds, lp, 6 ds, p, 6 ds, cl. Rw. Then make ch which forms lr outside circle as follows: Make ch of 6 ds, rw. With 2nd shuttle, make r of 6 ds, p, 6 ds, p, 6 ds, p, 6 ds, cl. Continue ch of 6 ds, p, 6 ds, p, 6 ds, rw. With 2nd shuttle, make r of 6 ds, 3 p's sep. by 6 ds, 6 ds, cl. Continue ch of 6 ds. Tie thread at base of inner r, thus forming lr outside circle, with r on both sides. Ch of 6 ds, join to last p of last r made, 6 ds, p, 6 ds, * rw. Inner r of 6 ds, p, 6 ds, join to lp of 1st inner r, 6 ds, p, 6 ds, cl, rw. Ch of 6 ds, rw. With 2nd shuttle make r of 6 ds, join to last p of previous ch, 6 ds, join to center p of adjacent r, 6 ds, p, 6 ds, cl. Rw and continue ch of 6 ds, p, 6 ds, p, 6 ds. Rw. With 2nd shuttle make r of 6 ds, p, 6 ds, p, 6 ds, p, 6 ds, cl. Rw. Ch of 6 ds. Tie thread securely at base of inner r. Ch of 6 ds, join to last p of last r made, 6 ds, p, 6 ds. Repeat from * 2 more times. Tie securely and cut off. Make 4 medallions for 1st row of corner, 3 for 2nd row, 2 for 3rd row, and 1 for last row, joining at the 2 p's between lr's outside circle, to adjacent 2 p's between lr's of adjacent medallion (see illustration).

Clover for Joinings: R of 6 ds, join to 2nd free p of lr outside circle, 4 ds, ** join to 1st p of lr of adjacent medallion, 6 ds, cl. Rw. R of 6 ds, join to 2nd p of same lr, 4 ds. Repeat from ** until clover is made. Tie securely and break off. Finish all other sps in same way.

Exquisite Luncheon Set
(Continued from page 30.)

Bread and Butter Plate Doily. 1st to 3rd rnds incl.: Work exactly as for first 3 rnds of place doily. **4th rnd:** * R of 8 ds, join to p of ch of previous rnd, 8 ds, cl. Rw. Ch of 5 ds, p, 6 ds, p, 5 ds. Rw. R of 8 ds, join to next p of ch, 8 ds, cl. Rw. Ch of 5 ds, p, 6 ds, p, 5 ds. Rw. R of 8 ds, join to next p, 8 ds, cl. Rw. Ch of 8 ds, p, 8 ds. Rw. R of 8 ds, join to next p, 8 ds, cl. Rw. Ch of 8 ds, p, 8 ds. Rw. Repeat from * around. Tie securely and cut off. **5th rnd:** * R of 8 ds, join to p of ch of previous rnd, 8 ds, cl. Rw. Ch of 8 ds, p, 8 ds. Repeat from * around. Tie securely and cut off. **6th rnd:** * R of 8 ds, join to p of previous rnd, 8 ds, cl. Rw. Ch of 5 ds, p, 2 ds, p, 2 ds, p, 5 ds. Rw. Repeat from * around. Tie securely and cut off. **Border.** Work exactly as for border of place doily.
Goblet Doily. 1st to 4th rnds incl: Same as 1st to 4th rnds incl. of bread and butter plate doily. Work border as before.

FINE EDGINGS

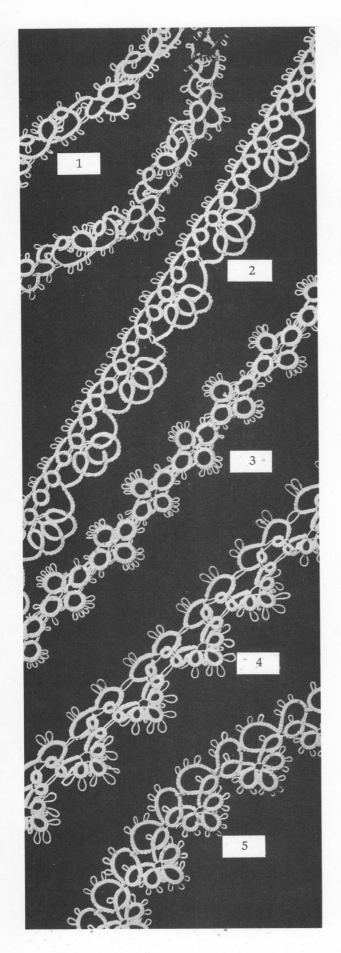

No. 1   Tie shuttle and ball threads. R of 4 ds, 3 p's sep. by 4 ds, 4 ds, cl. Rw, ch of 3 ds, 5 p's sep. by 3 ds, 3 ds, rw. * R of 3 ds, 3 p's sep. by 3 ds, 3 ds, join to 2nd p of last r, 3 ds, 4 p's sep. by 3 ds, 3 ds, cl. Rw, ch of 3 ds, 5 p's sep. by 3 ds, 3 ds, rw. R of 4 ds, p, 4 ds, join to lowest p of last r, 4 ds, p, 4 ds, cl. Rw, ch of 4 ds, p, 4 ds, rw. R of 4 ds, 5 p's sep. by 4 ds, 4 ds, cl. Rw, ch of 3 ds, p, 3 ds, join to 3rd p of last 5-p ch, 3 ds, p, 3 ds. Join to nearest p of last r and continue to make ch of 3 ds, 3 p's sep. by 3 ds, 3 ds. Join to next p of same r, ch of 3 ds, 3 p's sep. by 3 ds, 3 ds. Join to next p of r, ch of 4 ds, p, 4 ds. Rw, r of 4 ds, 3 p's sep. by 4 ds, 4 ds, cl. Rw, ch of 3 ds, p, 3 ds, join to 2nd p of last ch of 3 p's, 3 ds, 3 p's sep. by 3 ds, 3 ds, rw. Repeat from * for desired length.

No. 2   Tie shuttle and ball threads. **1st row:** R of 4 ds, 3 p's sep. by 4 ds, 4 ds, cl. * Rw, ch of 2 ds, 2 p's sep. by 2 ds, 2 ds, rw. R of 4 ds, join to last p of previous r, 8 ds, p, 4 ds, cl. Rw, ch as before, rw. R of 4 ds, join to last p of previous r, 3 ds, 3 p's sep. by 1 ds, 3 ds, p, 4 ds, cl. Rw, ch as before, rw. R of 4 ds, join to last p of previous r, 8 ds, p, 4 ds, cl. Rw, ch as before. Rw, r of 4 ds, join to last p of last r, 4 ds, 2 p's sep. by 4 ds, 4 ds, cl. Repeat from * for desired length. Tie ends and cut. **2nd row:** Tie threads to center p of last r made on 1st row. Ch of 8 ds, rw. * R of 10 ds, join to 1st of 3 p's on next 3-p r, 10 ds, cl. Rw, ch of 9 ds, rw. R of 12 ds, join to next p of same r, 12 ds, cl. Rw, ch of 9 ds, rw. R of 10 ds, join to next p of same r, 10 ds, cl. Rw, ch of 8 ds, skip 1 r, join to center p of next r, ch of 8 ds, rw. Repeat from * across. Tie ends and cut.

No. 3   Use one shuttle. Make r of 5 ds, p, 4 ds, 5 p's sep. by 2 ds, 4 ds, p, 5 ds, cl. * Sp (⅛-inch), r of 5 ds, join to p of lr, 4 ds, 5 p's sep. by 2 ds, 4 ds, p, 5 ds, cl. Repeat from * 2 more times, taking care to join the last lr at both sides. Tie ends together and cut. Make r of 5 ds, p, 4 ds, p, 2 ds, skip 1 p of one lr of previous piece, ** join to next p, 2 ds. Repeat from ** 2 more times, 2 ds, p, 4 ds, p, 5 ds, cl. Complete as for first piece. Continue thus for desired length.

No. 4   Tie shuttle and ball threads. **1st row:** Make a ch of 6 ds, 2 p's sep. by 2 ds, 5 ds, p, 5 ds, rw. R of 6 ds, p, 6 ds, cl. R of 4 ds, 2 p's sep. by 4 ds, 4 ds, cl. * Rw, ch of 6 ds, rw. R of 4 ds, join to last p of previous r, 3 ds, 3 p's sep. by 3 ds, 4 ds, cl. R of 4 ds, join to last p of last r, 3 ds, 4 p's sep. by 3 ds, 4 ds, cl. R of 4 ds, join to last p of last r, 3 ds, 3 p's sep. by 3 ds, 4 ds, cl (the last 3 rings form clover). Rw, ch of 6 ds, rw. R of 4 ds, join to last p of last r, 4 ds, p, 4 ds, cl. R of 6 ds, p, 6 ds, cl. Rw, ch of 6 ds, join to p of 1st ch, ch of 5 ds, 2 p's sep. by 2 ds, 6 ds, join to p of last r. Ch of 6 ds, 2 p's sep. by 2 ds, 5 ds, p, 5 ds, rw. R of 6 ds, join to same p where ch was joined, 6 ds, cl. R of 4 ds, join to p of next r, 4 ds, p, 4 ds, cl. Repeat from * for desired length. Tie ends and cut.

No. 5   Tie shuttle and ball threads. Ch of 6 ds, 3 p's sep. by 3 ds, 6 ds, p, 4 ds, rw. R of 4 ds, p, 6 ds, join to beginning of last ch, 6 ds, p, 4 ds, cl. * Rw, ch of 4 ds, rw. R of 4 ds, join to last p of previous r, 3 ds, 4 p's sep. by 3 ds, 4 ds, cl. R of 4 ds, join to last p of last r, 3 ds, 5 p's sep. by 3 ds, 4 ds, cl. R of 4 ds, join to last p of last r, 3 ds, 4 p's sep. by 3 ds, 4 ds, cl (clover). Rw, ch of 4 ds, rw. R of 4 ds, join to last p of last r, 6 ds, p, 6 ds, p, 4 ds, cl. Rw, ch of 4 ds, join to p of last p-ch, 6 ds, 3 p's sep. by 3 ds, 6 ds, join to center p of last r. Rw, ch of 6 ds, 3 p's sep. by 3 ds, 6 ds, p, 4 ds, rw. R of 4 ds, p, 6 ds, join to p of last r where ch was joined, 6 ds, p, 4 ds, cl. Repeat from * for desired length.

GIFT EDGINGS

Materials Required—AMERICAN THREAD COMPANY "STAR" MERCERIZED CROCHET COTTON

1—175 Yd. Ball, Size 50, will be required for each towel.

Star Twist Sewing Thread for Hemstitching and Hemming.

To make guest towels. Cut a piece of linen or linen finish material 13 x 20 inches (or size desired). Hemstitch the 2 ends and make a narrow hem on long sides using Star Twist in a matching color.

Hemstitching. Decide on the size hem desired and draw 5 or more threads. Baste a hem meeting the drawn threads. Working on the wrong side, and beginning at left of hem, pick up 4 or 5 threads (from right to left) pull needle through, tighten and make a second st in hem, pick up the next 4 or 5 threads, pull thread through and fasten with a second st in hem. Repeat till all threads are picked up. For a double hemstitch repeat on the other side of drawn threads.

Top

R, 8 d, p, 2 d, p, 8 d, cl r. R, 8 d, p, 2 d, p, 8 d, cl r, turn. Ch, 8 d, p, 8 d, turn. R, 8 d, join to p of 1st r, 2 d, p, 8 d, p, 2 d, cl r. R, 2 d, join to last p of last r, 8 d, 4 p sep by 2 d, 8 d, cl r, turn. * Ch, 8 d, turn. R, 2 d, join to 4th p of last r, 8 d, 3 p sep by 2 d, 8 d, p, 2 d, cl r, turn. Ch, 8 d, turn. R, 8 d, join to last p of last r, 2 d, 3 p sep by 2 d, 8 d, p, 2 d, cl r. R, 2 d, join to last p of last r, 8 d, p, 2 d, p, 8 d, cl r, turn. Ch, 8 d, join to p of opposite ch, 8 d, turn. R, 8 d, join to p of last r, 2 d, p, 8 d, cl r, turn. R, 8 d, join to p of opposite r, 2 d, p, 8 d, cl r, turn. Ch, 8 d, 3 p sep by 2 d, 8 d, turn. R, 8 d, join to p of opposite r, 2 d, p, 8 d, cl r, turn. R, 8 d, p, 2 d, p, 8 d, cl r, turn. Ch, 8 d, p, 8 d, turn. R, 8 d, join to 3rd r of group, 2 d, join to 1st r of group, 8 d, p, 2 d, cl r. R, 2 d, join to last p of last r, 8 d, 4 p sep by 2 d, 8 d, cl r and repeat from * for desired length.

Bottom

Use 2 Shuttles or 1 Shuttle and 1 Ball.

MOTIF

R, 2 d, 8 p sep by 3 d, 1 d, close r, tie and cut. R, 3 d, p, 3 d, join to p of large r, 3 d, p, 3 d, close r. ** Ch, 3 d. 5 p sep by 2 d, 3 d. * R, 3 d, join to 3rd p of last r made, 3 d, join to next p of center r, 3 d, p, 3 d, close r. Ch, 3 d, 5 p sep by 2 d, 3 d, repeat from *. R, 3 d, join to last p of last r made, 3 d, join to next p of center r, 3 d, p, 3 d, close r, turn. Ch, 5 d, p, 3 d, turn. R, 5 d, 3 p, sep by 5 d, 5 d, close r, turn. R, 5 d, join to last p of last r, 3 d, 5 p sep by 2 d, 3 d, p, 5 d, close r. R, 5 d, join to last p of last r, 5 d, p, 5 d, p, 5 d, close r, turn. Ch, 3 d, join to p of opposite ch, 5 d, turn. ** R, 3 d, join to last p of 4th r, 3 d, join to next p of center r, 3 d, p, 3 d, close r. Repeat between ** joining last p of 8th small r to 1st p of 1st small r, tie and cut thread.

Work 2 more motifs and applique to towel as illustrated.

EDGING

R, 6 d, 3 p sep by 3 d, 6 d, cl r, turn. Ch, 6 d, 3 p sep by 3 d, 6 d, turn. * R, 6 d, join to last p of last r, 3 d, p, 6 d, cl r, turn. Ch, 6 d, 3 p sep by 3 d, 6 d, turn. R, 6 d, join to p of small r, 6 d, join to center p of large r, 6 d, p, 6 d, cl r, turn. Ch, 6 d, 3 p sep by 3 d, 6 d, turn. R, 6 d, join to p of large r, 3 d, p, 6 d, cl r, turn. Ch, 6 d, 3 p sep by 3 d, 6 d, turn. R, 6 d, join to p of small r, 6 d, join to center p of large r, 6 d, p, 6 d, cl r, turn. Ch, 6 d, 3 p sep by 3 d, 6 d, turn. R, 6 d, 3 p sep by 6 d, 6 d, cl r. Ch, 6 d, join to 1st p on opposite ch, 2 d, join to next p of same ch, 3 d, p, 6 d, turn and repeat from * for desired length.

LACY TWIRL CHAIR SET

Materials Required—
AMERICAN THREAD COMPANY
"STAR" MERCERIZED CROCHET COTTON
Article 30, Size 50

6-150 yd. Balls White or Ecru.

1 Shuttle and 1 Ball.

Chair Back measures about 11½ x 15½ inches.

Arm Rest measures about 11½ x 5¼ inches.

ARM REST—R, 4 d, 3 p sep by 4 d, 4 d, cl r. Ch, 8 d, 3 p sep by 4 d, 8 d, turn. R, 4 d, join to last p of 1st r, 4 d, join to 2nd p of same r, 4 d, p, 4 d, cl r, turn. Ch, 8 d, 3 p sep by 4 d, 8 d, turn. R, 4 d, join to last p of last r made, 4 d, join to center p of 1st r, 4 d, p, 4 d, cl r, turn. Ch, 8 d, p, 8 d. * R, 4 d, 3 p sep by 4 d, 4 d, cl r, turn. Ch, 8 d, 3 p sep by 4 d, 8 d, join to center p of last r made, 8 d, 3 p sep by 4 d, 8 d, turn. R, 4 d, p, 4 d, join to center p of last r made, 4 d, p, 4 d, cl r, turn. Repeat from * 12 times, turn. R, 4 d, 3 p sep by 4 d, 4 d, cl r, turn. Ch, 8 d, 3 p sep by 4 d, 8 d, turn. R, 4 d, join to last p of last r, 4 d, join to center p of same r, 4 d, p, 4 d, cl r, turn. Ch, 8 d, 3 p sep by 4 d, 8 d, turn. R, 4 d, join to last p of last r, 4 d, join to center p of opposite r, 4 d, p, 4 d, cl r, turn. * Ch, 8 d, p, 8 d. R, 4 d, 3 p sep by 4 d, 4 d, cl r, turn. Ch, 8 d, p, 4 d,

join to center p of opposite ch, 4 d, p, 8 d, join to center p of last r made, 8 d, p, 4 d, join to center p of opposite ch, 4 d, p, 8 d, turn. R, 4 d, p, 4 d, join to center p of last r made, 4 d, p, 4 d, cl r, turn. Repeat from * 12 times. Ch, 8 d, p, 8 d, tie and cut.

2nd Strip—R, 4 d, 3 p sep by 4 d, 4 d, cl r. Ch, 8 d, 3 p sep by 4 d, 8 d, turn. R, 4 d, join to last p of 1st r, 4 d, join to 2nd p of same r, 4 d, p, 4 d, cl r, turn. Ch, 8 d, 3 p sep by 4 d, 8 d, turn. R, 4 d, join to last p of last r made, 4 d, join to center p of same r, 4 d, p, 4 d, cl r, turn. * Ch, 8 d, join to corresponding p of 1st strip, 8 d. R, 4 d, join to corresponding p of opposite r of 1st strip, 4 d, 2 p sep by 4 d, 4 d, cl r, turn. Ch, 8 d, 3 p sep by 4 d, 8 d, join to center p of last r made, 8 d, 3 p sep by 4 d, 8 d, turn. R, 4 d, p, 4 d, join to same center p of last r, 4 d, join to corresponding p of opposite r of 1st strip, 4 d, cl r. Repeat from * 12 times. Ch, 8 d, join to corresponding p of opposite ch, 8 d, complete strip same as 1st strip. Work 4 more strips joining all strips in same manner.

Work another arm rest in same manner.

Chair Back—Work 18 strips same as arm rest joining all strips in same manner.

SHEER BEAUTY

Right Doily

Materials: Clark's O.N.T. or J. & P. Coats Mercerized Crochet, size 30, White or Ecru, 1 ball.
A shuttle.
¼ yd. linen.

When completed, doily measures about 11 inches in diameter.

Cut a circle of linen 8 inches in diameter and make a narrow hem all around edge. Starting at one of the r's sewed to linen center, make r of 6 ds, p, 5 ds, p, 6 ds, cl. Rw and make similar r, close to 1st r. Rw, ch of 8 ds, p, 8 ds. Rw; make r (all r's and all ch's are alike), join to last p of adjacent r. Rw and make similar r close to this r. Rw and make a ch. Rw, make r, joining 1st p to last p of last r. Rw, make a ch. * Make 4 more r's, sep. by ch's, joining each to preceding r, also joining the 4th r by its last p to free p of adjacent r (thus forming a circle of 6 r's). Rw, make similar r close to last r. Rw, ch, joined by p to p of adjacent ch. Rw, r, joining last p to free p of r just made. Rw, a similar r close to last r, joining by its 1st p to free p of 1st r made. Ch as before (inner edge). R, joining 1st p to last p of adjacent r. Rw, similar r close to r just made. Rw and make a ch. Rw, r, joining to 2 adjacent r's. Rw, similar r close to last r. Ch, joining to p of opposite ch. Rw, r, joining to preceding r. Repeat from * for length desired, joining last scallop to 1st.
Sew inner edge to linen.

Left Doily

Materials: Clark's O.N.T. or J. & P. Coats Mercerized Crochet, size 30, White, 1 ball.
A shuttle.

When completed, doily measures about 5 inches in diameter.

Center Medallion. Starting at center, make sr of 4 ds, 5 p's sep. by 3 ds, 4 ds, cl. Sr of 4 ds, join to last p of previous r, 3 ds, 4 p's sep. by 3 ds, 4 ds, cl. Make another r same as last r, cl. R of 4 ds, join to last p of previous r, 3 ds, p, 3 ds, p, 3 ds, p, 3 ds, join to 1st p of 1st sr, 4 ds, cl. Tie securely and cut off. **1st rnd:** * Sr of 4 ds, p, 4 ds, join to last of 3 free p's of center r, 4 ds, join to 1st free p of next center r, 4 ds, p, 4 ds, cl. Rw. Attach ball thread, ch of 4 ds, 7 p's sep. by 2 ds, 4 ds. Rw, lr of 4 ds, p, 4 ds, p, 4 ds, join to next center p of center r, 4 ds, p, 4 ds, p, 4 ds, cl. Rw, make a ch as before. Repeat from * around, joining last ch to sr first made. Tie securely and cut off. **2nd**

(Continued on next page.)

CHAIR BACK

Materials: Clark's O.N.T. or J. & P. Coats Mercerized Crochet, size 20, 3 balls and a shuttle.

Each motif measures about 4¾ inches in diameter.

Chair Back. Tie ends of shuttle and ball threads together. Make center r of 6 ds, p, 6 ds, cl. Rw and on ball thread make ch of 3 ds, p, 3 ds, p, 3 ds, p, 3 ds. Rw and repeat from beginning 5 more times. Join last ch close to 1st r and fasten off. With a needle run a thread through each of the picots, tie firmly and fasten off. **1st rnd:** R of 6 ds, join to 3rd p of 1st ch, 6 ds, cl, rw. On ball thread make ch of 3 ds, p, 3 ds, p, 3 ds, p, 3 ds. Continue around, joining r's to 1st and 3rd p's of each ch of center medallion (12 r's and 12 ch's). Break off. **2nd rnd:** Same as 1st rnd, joining r's to 1st and 3rd p's of each ch. In this rnd the r's are 3 ds, p, 3 ds, join to p of ch, 3 ds, p, 3 ds, cl. Join p's of adjacent r's. **3rd rnd:** Make r's of 6 ds, join to center p of ch of previous rnd, 6 ds, cl, rw. On ball thread make ch of 3 ds, and 5 p's sep. by 3 ds, 3 ds. Break off. **4th rnd:** Work same as 3rd rnd, making ch of 6 ds, 5 p's sep. by 2 ds, 6 ds. Fasten and break off. This completes one medallion. Make 4 more medallions and join as shown in illustration. If arm pieces are desired, two joined medallions for each arm can be made.

Many other adaptations of this lovely design can be made. Separate medallions can be used for doilies—and the design is effective for a luncheon set, omitting the last two rounds for the glass doilies and adding rounds as desired for the plate doilies.

The medallions are also attractively used as insets in linen for table runners, dresser scarfs, or luncheon sets.

Sheer Beauty
(Continued from page 36.)

rnd: * Sr of 4 ds, p, 4 ds, join to last p of ch of 2nd rnd, 4 ds, join to 1st p of next ch, 4 ds, p, 4 ds, cl. Rw, ch of 3 ds, 7 p's sep. by 2 ds, 3 ds, rw. Lr of 4 ds, p, 4 ds, p, 4 ds, sk 2 p's of ch, join to next p, 4 ds, p, 4 ds, p, 4 ds, cl. Rw, make a ch as before. Repeat from * around, joining last ch to 1st sr made. This completes center medallion.

Small Medallion. Starting at center, lr of 2 ds, 8 p's sep. by 3 ds, 1 ds, cl. Tie securely and cut off. * Make r of 4 ds, p, 4 ds, join to p of center r, 4 ds, p, 4 ds, cl. Rw. Attach ball thread, ch of 3 ds, 5 p's sep. by 2 ds, 3 ds, rw. R of 4 ds, join to last p of previous r, 4 ds, join to next p of center r, 4 ds, p, 4 ds, cl. Rw. Make a ch as before. Repeat from * around, joining center p of each of 2 ch's to center p of ch's on center medallion, and joining last ch to r first made. Make 7 more medallions same as this, but joining the center p of ch to center p of ch on previous medallion, and taking care to join the last medallion at center p of adjacent medallions.

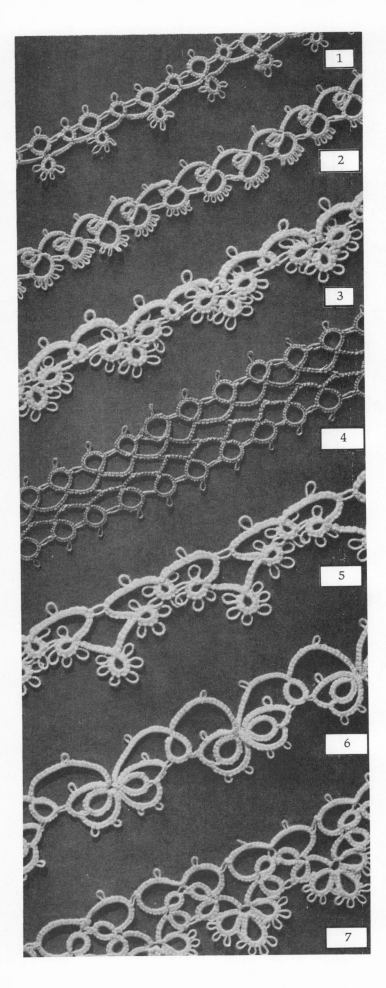

DAINTY

For finest results use:
J. & P. Coats Tatting Cotton, Clark's O.N.T. or

No. 1

Use one shuttle and a ball of thread. Tie ends of shuttle and ball threads together. With shuttle thread, r of 3 ds, 3 p's sep. by 2 ds, 3 ds, cl. * Rw and on ball thread make ch of 7 ds, rw. R of 3 ds, 4 p's sep. by 2 ds, 3 ds, cl. Rw. Lr of 5 ds, join to p of 1st r, 5 ds, p, 5 ds, p, 5 ds, cl. Rw and on ball thread make ch of 7 ds, rw. R of 3 ds, join to side p of lr, 2 ds, p, 2 ds, p, 3 ds, cl. Repeat from * for length desired.

No. 2

Use one shuttle and a ball of thread. Tie ends of shuttle and ball threads together. With shuttle thread, sr of 6 ds, p, 6 ds, cl. Lr of 6 ds, join to p of r just made. 3 ds, 5 p's sep. by 2 ds, 3 ds, p, 3 ds, cl. * Rw and on ball thread make ch of 8 ds, p, 5 ds, rw. Sr of 6 ds, p, 6 ds, cl. Lr of 6 ds, join to p of r just made, 3 ds, join to side p of lr, 2 ds, 5 p's sep. by 2 ds, 3 ds, p, 3 ds, cl. Repeat from * for length desired.

No. 3

Use one shuttle and a ball of thread. Tie ends of shuttle and ball threads. R of 3 ds, p, 3 ds, p, 3 ds, cl. * Rw and make a ch of 5 ds, p, 5 ds, p, 3 ds, rw. R of 2 ds, p, 2 ds, p, 2 ds, join to adjacent p of 1st r, 2 ds, 3 p's sep. by 2 ds, 2 ds, cl. R of 2 ds, join to last p of previous r, 2 ds, 5 p's sep. by 2 ds, 2 ds, cl. R of 2 ds, join to last p of previous r, 2 ds, 5 p's sep. by 2 ds, 2 ds, cl. Rw and on ball thread make ch of 3 ds, join to 2nd p of previous ch, 5 ds, p, 5 ds, rw. R of 3 ds, skip 2 p's of 3rd r of top motif, join to next, 3 ds, p, 3 ds, cl. Repeat from * for length desired.

No. 4

Use one shuttle and a ball of thread.
R of 6 ds, p, 6 ds, p, 6 ds, p, 6 ds, cl. * Rw, ch of 6 ds, p, 6 ds, rw. R of 6 ds, join to side p of previous r, 6 ds, p, 6 ds, p, 6 ds, cl. Repeat from * for desired length. This completes one-half of insertion. For other half, work same as this but join to first half at the p's of ch's.

No. 5

Use one shuttle and a ball of thread. Tie the shuttle and ball threads together. Starting at center of lower 3-r group, r of 2 ds, 5 p's sep. by 2 ds, 2 ds, cl. * Rw and on ball thread make ch of 6 ds, p, 6 ds, p, 6 ds, rw. R of 2 ds, p, 2 ds, skip 1 p of r just made, join to next p, make 3 more p's sep. by 2 ds, 2 ds, cl. Rw and on ball thread make ch of 6 ds, rw. R of 2 ds, 6 p's sep. by 2 ds, 2 ds, cl. Rw and on ball thread make ch of 6 ds, rw. R of 2 ds, 5 p's sep. by 2 ds, 2 ds, cl. Rw and on ball thread make ch of 6 ds, join to 2nd p of previous ch, 6 ds, p, 6 ds. Rw, r of 2 ds, p, 2 ds, skip 1 p of adjacent r, join to next p, 2 ds, 3 p's sep. by 2 ds, 2 ds, cl. Repeat from * for length desired.

Directions for Nos. 6 and 7 on page 40.

EDGINGS

J. & P. Coats Mercerized Crochet.

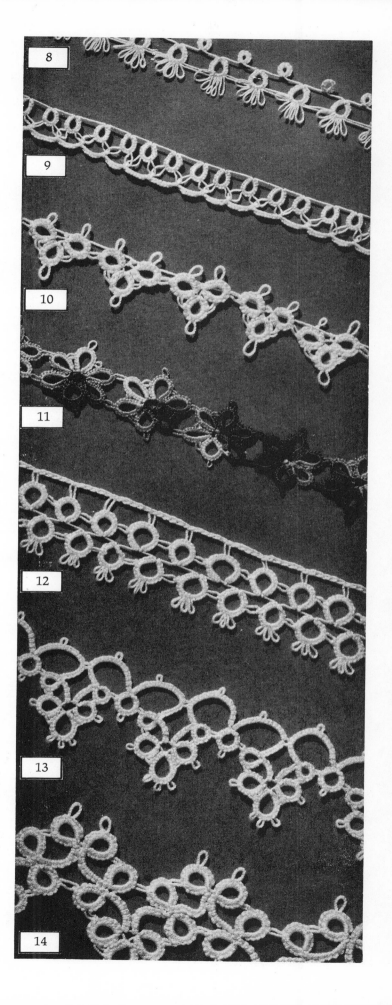

No. 8

R of 7 ds, lp, * 5 p's sep. by 1 ds, lp, 7 ds, cl. Sp (¼-inch), rw. R of 10 ds, cl. Sp (¼-inch), rw. R of 7 ds, join to lp of 1st r. Repeat from * for length desired.

No. 9

Use one shuttle and a ball of thread.
* R of 6 ds, p, 4 ds, p, 6 ds, cl. Sp (¼-inch). Repeat from * for length desired. Then attach ball thread to 1st p of 1st r. **Make a ch of 10 ds on ball thread, join to 2 p's (2nd p of 1st r and 1st p of adjacent r). Repeat from ** across entire length.

No. 10

R of 4 ds, p, 4 ds, p, 4 ds, p, 4 ds, cl. * R close to ring just made of 4 ds, join to side of p of 1st r, 4 ds, p, 4 ds, p, 4 ds, cl. R of 4 ds close to r just made, join to side p of 2nd r, 4 ds, p, 4 ds, p, 4 ds, cl. Knot these 3 rings into cluster. Sp (¾-inch). R of 4 ds, p, 4 ds, join to center p of 3rd r, 4 ds, p, 4 ds, cl. Repeat from * for length desired.

No. 11

R of 4 ds, p, 4 ds, p, 4 ds, p, 4 ds, cl. Make 5 more r's same as this close together, but joining them together at the side p of previous r. Fasten and break off. This completes one flower. Make as many flowers as necessary for length desired, but join each flower to the previous one at the center p's of the 2 r's while completing the flower.

No. 12

Use a shuttle and Milward's steel crochet hook.
R of 5 ds, p, 4 ds, p, 4 ds, p, 5 ds, cl. Rw. Sp (¼-inch), r of 5 ds, p, 3 ds, 3 p's sep. by 1 ds, 3 ds, p, 5 ds, cl. * Rw. Sp (¼-inch), r of 5 ds, join to p of adjacent r, 4 ds, p, 4 ds, p, 5 ds, cl. Rw. Sp (¼-inch), r of 5 ds, join to p of adjacent r, 3 ds, 3 p's sep. by 1 ds, 3 ds, p, 5 ds, cl. Repeat from * for length desired. Attach thread to center p of 1st r made, ** ch 5, s c in free p of next r. Repeat from ** across. Break off.

No. 13

Use one shuttle and a ball of thread. Tie ends of shuttle and ball threads together. * R of 4 ds, p, 4 ds, p, 4 ds, p, 4 ds, cl. Rw and on ball thread make ch of 7 ds, p, 7 ds, p, 5 ds. Rw. R of 4 ds, join to 3rd p of 1st r, 4 ds, p, 4 ds, cl. Rw, ch of 5 ds, rw. R of 4 ds, join to p of 2nd r, 4 ds, p, 4 ds, p, 4 ds, cl. Lr of 4 ds, join to p of r just made, 4 ds, p, 2 ds, p, 2 ds, p, 4 ds, p, 4 ds, cl. R same as 3rd r, joining to last p of r just made. Rw, ch of 5 ds, rw, and make r like 2nd, joining to p of adjacent r. Rw and on ball thread make ch of 5 ds, join to p of adjacent ch, 7 ds, p, 7 ds. Repeat from * for length desired, joining r to p of adjacent r of motif.

Directions for No. 14 on page 40.

No. 6

Use one shuttle and a ball of thread. With shuttle thread, make lr of 8 ds, p, 4 ds, p, 8 ds, cl. Attach ball thread. * Rw, ch of 10 ds, p, 10 ds. Rw and with shuttle thread make r of 9 ds, p, 9 ds, cl (inner r made). Rw and with shuttle thread ch of 8 ds, p, 4 ds, join to last p of 1st r made, 4 ds, join to p of inner r, 4 ds, p, 4 ds, p, 8 ds. Join to base of inner r. Rw and with shuttle thread make another inner r as before. Rw, ch of 8 ds, p, 4 ds, p, 4 ds, join to p of last inner r, 4 ds, p, 4 ds, p, 8 ds. Join to base of last inner r. Ch of 10 ds, p, 10 ds. Rw and with shuttle thread make r of 8 ds, join to 2nd p of 4-p ch, 4 ds, p, 8 ds, cl. Repeat from * for length desired.

No. 7

Use one shuttle and a ball of thread.

Make a ch of 7 ds, p, 7 ds, rw. With shuttle thread, sr of 7 ds, p, 7 ds, cl. Sr of 6 ds, p, 2 ds, p, 6 ds, cl. * Rw. Make a ch of 7 ds, rw. With shuttle thread, lr of 4 ds, join to last p of sr, 3 ds, 3 p's sep. by 2 ds, 3 ds, p, 4 ds, cl. Lr of 5 ds, join to last p of previous lr, 3 ds, 3 p's sep. by 2 ds, 3 ds, p, 5 ds, cl. Lr of 4 ds, join to last p of lr, 3 ds, 3 p's sep. by 2 ds, 3 ds, p, 4 ds, cl. Rw. Make a ch of 7 ds, rw. With shuttle thread, sr of 6 ds, join to last p of lr, 2 ds, p, 6 ds, cl. R of 7 ds, p, 7 ds, cl. Rw. Make a ch of 7 ds, join to p of 1st ch made, 7 ds, p, 7 ds, join to p of last sr, ch of 7 ds, p, 7 ds, p, 7 ds. With shuttle thread, sr of 7 ds, join in same p as previous joining, 7 ds, cl. Sr of 7 ds, join to p where sr was joined to lr, 2 ds, p, 7 ds, cl. Repeat from * for length desired.

No. 14

Use one shuttle and a ball of thread. Tie ends of shuttle and ball threads together. * R of 6 ds, p, 6 ds, p, 6 ds, cl. Rw and on ball thread make ch of 8 ds. Rw, make r like 1st, joining to 2nd p of 1st r. Rw, make another r like 1st. Rw and on ball thread, make ch of 8 ds, rw. Make r as before, joining to adjacent p of 3rd r. Close to 4th r make r of 6 ds, join to 2nd p of 4th r, 6 ds, p, 6 ds, p, 6 ds, cl. Close to 5th r, make another r like 4th, joining to last p of r just made. Rw and make ch of 8 ds. R as before, joining to last p of 2nd r made. Rw, another r, joining to last p of 6th r. Ch of 8 ds, rw and make r as before, joining to p of 7th r. Repeat from * for length desired, joining 3rd r to last p of 8th r of 1st motif.

ANEMONE

Materials Required — AMERICAN THREAD COMPANY "STAR" MERCERIZED CROCHET COTTON

2—175 Yd. Balls—Size 50 White.

Doily measures about 7 inches.

1 Shuttle and 1 Ball.

1st Row. L r, 7 d, 6 p sep by 3 d, 7 d, cl r. * R, 7 d, join to 6th p of last r, 3 d, 5 p sep by 3 d, 7 d, cl r. Repeat from * twice, join to 1st r, tie and cut.

2nd Row. R, 4 d, join to p of r in 1st row, 4 d, cl r, turn. Ch, 5 d, p, 5 d, turn. * R, 4 d, join to next p of r, 4 d, cl r, turn. Ch, 5 d, p, 5 d, turn and repeat from * until all picots have been joined.

3rd Row. R, 3 d, 3 p sep by 3 d, 3 d, cl r. R,

3 d, join to 3rd p of last r, 3 d, p, 3 d join to p of ch in 2nd row, 3 d, 2 p sep by 3 d, 3 d, cl r. R, 3 d, join to 5th p of last r, 3 d, 2 p sep by 3 d, 3 d, cl r, turn. * Ch, 5 d, 3 p sep by 2 d, 5 d, turn. R, 3 d, p, 3 d, join to next p of 2nd row, 3 d, p, 3 d, cl r. Repeat from * twice, turn. Ch, 5 d, 3 p sep by 2 d, 5 d. Repeat from beginning all around, tie and cut.

4th Row. R, 1 d, 4 p sep by 1 d, 1 d, join to center p of ch in 3rd row, 1 d, 4 p sep by 1 d, 1 d, cl r, turn. Ch, 5 d, 5 p sep by 2 d, 5 d, turn. R, 1 d, 4 p sep by 1 d, 1 d, join to 1st p of next ch in 3rd row, 1 d, 4 p sep by 1 d, 1 d, cl r, turn. Ch, 5 d, 5 p sep by 2 d, 5 d, turn. R, 1 d, 4 p sep by 1 d, 1 d, join to 3rd p of same ch in 3rd row, 1 d, 4 p sep by 1 d, 1 d,

(Continued on page 45.)

FRAGRANCE

Materials Required—AMERICAN THREAD COMPANY "STAR" MERCERIZED TATTING COTTON

4—75 Yd.. Balls White or Colors.

Doily measures about 7½ x 11½.

1st Row. R, 3 d, 7 p sep by 3 d, 3 d, close r. R, 3 d, join to last p of 1st r, 3 d, join to 2nd p of same r, 3 d, 7 p sep by 3 d, 3 d, close r. R, 3 d, join to last p of last r, 3 d, join to next p of same r, 3 d, 5 p sep by 3 d, 3 d, close r. Ch, 6 d. * R, 3 d, join to 1st p of last r, 3 d, 6 p sep by 3 d, 3 d, close r, turn. R, 3 d, join to last p of r on opposite side, 3 d, 6 p sep by 3 d, 3 d, close r. Ch, 6 d and repeat from * until there are 19 rings on each side and work corner ring same as opposite end, break thread.

2nd Row. Join to center p of any r, ch, 3 d, p, 3 d, p, 3 d, p, 3 d, join in center p of next r and repeat chs all around, joining chs in the 1st, 3rd d and 5th p of end r, break thread.

3rd Row. R, 3 d, 5 p sep by 3 d, 3 d, close r, turn. * Ch, 3 d, p, 3 d, join to center p of 3rd ch from end, 3 d, p, 3 d, turn. R, 3 d, p, 3 d, join to 2nd p of last r, 3 d, 3 p sep by 3 d, 3 d, close r, turn and repeat from * 18 times. R, 3 d, join to last p of last r, 3 d, 4 p sep by 3 d, 3 d, close r, turn. Ch, 3 d, p, 3 d, join to 1st p of next ch, 3 d, p, 3 d, turn. R, 3 d, p, 3 d, join to 4th p of last r, 3 d, 3 p sep by 3 d, 3 d, close r, turn. Ch, 3 d, p, 3 d, join to 3rd p of ch in 2nd row, 3 d, p, 3 d, turn. R, 3 d, p, 3 d, join to 4th p of last r, 3 d, 3 p sep by 3 d, 3 d, close r, turn. Ch, 3 d, p, 3 d, join to 1st p of next ch, 3 d, p, 3 d, turn. R, 3 d, p, 3 d, join to 4th p of last r, 3 d, 3 p sep by 3 d, 3 d, close r, turn. Ch, 3 d, p, 3 d, join to 3rd p of same ch, 3 d, p, 3 d, turn. R, 3 d, p, 3 d, join to 4th p of last r, 3 d, 3 p sep by 3 d, 3 d, close r. R, 3 d, join to

last p of last r, 3 d, 4 p sep by 3 d, 3 d, close r, turn. Ch, 3 d, p, 3 d, join to center p of next ch, 3 d, p, 3 d, turn and repeat from beginning for other side.

4th Row. Repeat 2nd row.

5th Row. Work same as 3rd row but do not join rings together and increase twice at each end by joining into the 1st and 3rd p of chs same as in 3rd row, break thread.

6th Row. * R, 3 d, p, 3 d, join to 2nd p of any r, 3 d, p, 3 d, join to 4th p of next r, 3 d, p, 3 d, close r, turn. Ch, 3 d, p, 3 d, p, 3 d, p, 3 d, turn, repeat from * all around.

7th Row. Same as 5th row working chs of 6 d, join, 6 d and increasing twice on each end by joining in the 1st and 3rd p of ch.

8th Row. Repeat the 6th row with chs of 9 d, p, 9 d, break thread.

9th Row. Join to any loop. Ch, 6 d, p, 3 d, p, 3 d, p, 6 d, join to next loop and repeat all around, break thread.

10th Row. R, 3 d, 6 p sep by 3 d, 3 d, close r. * R, 3 d, join to last p of last r, 3 d, 6 p sep by 3 d, 3 d, close r. R, 3 d, join to last p of last r, 3 d, 5 p sep by 3 d, 3 d, close r, turn. Ch, 9 d, p, 9 d, turn. R, 3 d, p, 3 d, p, 3 d, join to 3rd free p of last r made, 3 d, p, 3 d, p, 3 d, p, 3 d, close r. R, 3 d, join to last p of last r, 3 d, 6 p, sep by 3 d, 3 d, close r. R, 3 d, join to last p of last r, 3 d, 5 p sep by 3 d, 3 d, close r, turn. Ch, 9 d, p, 9 d, p, 9 d, p, 9 d, join to center p of side loop in 9th row, 9 d, turn. R, 3 d, p, 3 d, join to 3rd p of last r made, 3 d, 3 p sep by 3 d, 3 d, close r, turn. Ch, 9 d, join to center p of next loop, 9 d, turn. R, 3 d, p, 3 d,

(Continued on page 45.)

LAVENDER & LACE

Materials Required—AMERICAN THREAD COMPANY "STAR" MERCERIZED CROCHET COTTON

13—175 Yd. Balls, Size 50, White.

1 Ball and a Shuttle are used.

35 Motifs 5 x 7 are required for each Plate Doily.

65 Motifs 5 x 13 are required for Center Doily.

Motif. 1st Row. R, 3 d, p, 3 d, p, 3 d, p, 3 d, close r, turn. * Ch, 6 d, p, 3 d, p, 3 d, p, 6 d, turn. R, 3 d, join to 3rd p of 1st r, 3 d, p, 3 d, p, 3 d, close r, turn, repeat from * 7 times joining to form circle.

2nd Row. R, 3 d, 5 p sep by 3 d, 3 d, close r. * R, 3 d, join to last p of 1st r, 3 d, 6 p sep by 3 d, 3 d, close r. R, 3 d, join to last p of 2nd r, 3 d, 4 p sep by 3 d, 3 d, close r, turn. Ch, 6 d, turn. R, 3 d, p, join to 2nd p of last r, 3 d, 3 p sep by 3 d, 3 d, close r, turn. Ch, 6 d, p, 6 d, join to 3rd p of any ch of 1st row, 6 d, join to 1st p of next ch of 1st row, 6 d, p, 6 d, turn. R, 3 d, p,

3 d, p, 3 d, join to 2nd p of last r made, 3 d, p, 3 d, p, 3 d, close r, turn. Ch, 6 d, turn. R, 3 d, 5 p sep by 3 d, 3 d, close r. Ch, 6 d, turn. R, 3 d, 5 p sep by 3 d, 3 d, close r, turn. Ch, 6 d, join to opposite p, 6 d, join to 3rd p of ch of 1st row, 6 d, join to 1st p of next ch of 1st row, 6 d, p, 6 d, turn. R, 3 d, p, 3 d, join to center p of last r made, 3 d, p, 3 d, p, 3 d, p, 3 d, close r, turn. Ch, 6 d, turn. R, 3 d, p, 3 d, join to 2nd p of last r made, 3 d, p, 3 d, p, 3 d, p, 3 d, close r and repeat from * all around, join.

2nd Motif. Repeat 1st row of 1st motif.

2nd Row. R, 3 d, 5 p sep by 3 d, 3 d, close r. R, 3 d, join to last p of last r, 3 d, 3 p sep by 3 d, 3 d, join to 2nd free p of corner r of 1st motif, 3 d, p, 3 d, p, 3 d, close r. R, 3 d, join to last p of last r, 3 d, 4 p sep by 3 d, 3 d, close r, turn. Ch, 6 d, turn. R, 3 d, p, 3 d, join to 2nd free p of last r, 3 d, 3 p sep by 3 d, 3 d, close r, turn. Ch, 6 d, p, 6 d, join to 3rd p of ch in 1st row, 3 d,

(Continued on page 45.)

43

ROSEGLOW

LUNCHEON SET

Materials Required—AMERICAN THREAD COMPANY "STAR" MERCERIZED CROCHET COTTON

5—175 Yd. Balls, Size 50, White.
½ Yd. of 36 inch Linen.
The hemmed circle in plate doilies measures 6 inches and the center doily 7½ inches.
1 Ball and 1 Shuttle are used for Tatting.

PLATE DOILY—

1st Row. R, 4 d, 5 p sep by 2 d, 4 d, close r, turn. * Ch, 4 d, p, 2 d, p, 2 d, p, 4 d, turn. R, 4 d, join to 5th p of 1st r, 2 d, 4 p sep by 2 d, 4 d, close r, turn. Repeat from * until there are 72 rings or for desired length having an even number of rings, join.

Anemone

(Continued from page 41.)

cl r, turn. Ch, 5 d, 5 p sep by 2 d, 5 d, turn. Repeat from beginning all around, tie and cut.

5th Row. * S R, 4 d, p, 4 d, cl r. L R, 4 d, join to p of s r, 4 d, join to center p of ch in last row, 4 d, p, 4 d, cl r. S R, 4 d, join to 3rd p of large r, 4 d, cl r, turn. Ch, 5 d, 5 p sep by 2 d, 5 d, turn. Repeat from * all around, tie and cut.

6th Row. R, 2 d, p, 2 d, join to center p of ch in last row, 2 d, p, 2 d, cl r, turn. * Ch, 5 d, p, 5 d, turn. R, 2 d, p, 2 d, join to 3rd p of last r, 2 d, p, 2 d, close r. R, 2 d, 3 p sep by 2 d, 2 d, cl r, turn. Ch, 5 d, p, 5 d, turn. R, 2 d, join to center p of last r, 2 d, join to center p of next ch, 2 d, p, 2 d, cl r, turn and repeat from * all around, tie and cut.

Motifs around Doily.

1st Row. R, 7 d, 5 p sep by 3 d, 7 d, cl r. * R, 7 d, join to 5th p of last r, 3 d, 4 p sep by 3 d, 7 d, cl r, repeat from * twice, join last r to 1st r, tie and cut.

2nd Row. * R, 3 d, p, 3 d, join to 1st free p of r in 1st row, 3 d, p, 3 d, cl r, turn. Ch, 5 d, 3 p sep by 2 d, 5 d, turn. S R, 3 d, 3 p sep by 3 d, 3 d, cl r. L R, 3 d, join to 3rd p of s r, 3 d, p, 3 d, join to next p of same r of 1st row, 3 d, 2 p sep by 3 d, 3 d, cl r. S R, 3 d, join to 5th p of large r, 3 d, 2 p sep by 3 d, 3 d, cl r. Ch, 5 d, 3 p sep by 2 d, 5 d, turn. R, 3 d, p, 3 d, join to next p of same large r of 1st row, 3 d, p, 3 d, cl r. Ch, 5 d, 3 p sep by 2 d, 5 d, turn. Repeat from * all around. Join center p of ch between the r and shamrock to center p of ch of last row and the center p of ch between the same shamrock and next r to the center p of next ch in last row, tie and cut.

Join the next motif to last motif in same manner. Skip 2 chs of last row between each motif.

Fragrance

(Continued from page 42.)

join to 2nd p of last r, 3 d, 3 p sep by 3 d, 3 d, close r, turn. Ch, 9 d, join to center p of next loop, 9 d, turn. R, 3 d, p, 3 d, join to 2nd p of last r, 3 d, 3 p sep by 3 d, 3 d, close r, turn. Ch, 9 d, join to center p of next loop, 9 d, p, 9 d, p, 9 d, p, 9 d, turn. R, 3 d, p, 3 d, p, 3 d, join to 2nd p of last r, 3 d, 3 p sep by 3 d, 3 d, close r. R, 3 d, join to p of last r, 3 d, p, 3 d, p, 3 d, join to center p of corresponding r, 3 d, 3 p sep by 3 d, 3 d, close r. R, 3 d, join to p of last r, 3 d, 5 p sep by 3 d, 3 d, close r, turn. Ch, 9 d, p, 9 d, turn and repeat from * increasing 4 scallops at each end by joining in the 1st and 3rd p of ch.

Lavender and Lace

(Continued from page 43.)

join to 1st p of next ch, 6 d, p, 6 d, turn. R, 3 d, p, 3 d, p, 3 d, join to 2nd free p of last r, 3 d, p, 3 d, p, 3 d, close r, turn. Ch, 6 d, join to center p of free r of 1st motif, 6 d. R, 3 d, 5 p sep by 3 d, 3 d, close r, turn. Ch, 6 d, join to p of opposite ch, 6 d, join to 3rd p of ch in 1st row, 6 d, join to 1st p of next ch in 1st row, 6 d, p, 6 d, turn. R, 3 d, p, 3 d, join to center p of last r, 3 d, 3 p sep by 3 d, 3 d, close r, turn. Ch, 6 d, turn. R, 3 d, p, 3 d, join to 2nd free p of last r, 3 d, 3 p sep by 3 d, 3 d, close r. R, 3 d, join to last p of last r, 3 d, p, 3 d, join to 2nd free p of corner r in 1st motif, 3 d, 4 p sep by 3 d, 3 d, close r. Complete motif same as 1st motif.

Join all motifs in same manner, always working rings in center sides of one motif and joining chs at sides to be joined on next motif.

Roseglow

(Continued from page 44.)

2nd Row. R, 4 d, 5 p sep by 2 d, 4 d, close r, turn. Ch, 4 d, p, 2 d, join to center p of any r of 1st row, 2 d, p, 4 d, turn. * R, 4 d, 5 p sep by 2 d, 4 d, close r, turn. Ch, 4 d, p, 2 d, join to center p of next r in 1st row, 2 d, p, 4 d, turn and repeat from * all around.

3rd Row. * R, 4 d, p, 2 d, join to 2nd p of any r in 2nd row, 2 d, p, 2 d, join to 4th p of next r, 2 d, p, 4 d, close r, turn. Ch, 6 d, p, 3 d, p, 3 d, p, 6 d, turn and repeat from * all around.

4th Row. R, 3 d, 5 p sep by 3 d, 3 d, close r, turn. Ch, 3 d, p, 3 d, p, 3 d, p, 3 d, turn. R, 3 d, 5 p sep by 3 d, 3 d, close r, turn. Ch 3 d, 5 p sep by 3 d, 3 d, join to center p of ch in 3rd row, 3 d, p, 3 d, p, 3 d, turn. * R, 3 d, p, 3 d, join to the 2nd p of last r made, 3 d join to the center p of same r, 3 d, p, 3 d, p, 3 d, close r. Ch, 3 d, p, 3 d, p, 3 d, join to center p of next ch in 3rd row, 3 d, 5 p sep by 3 d, 3 d, turn. R, 3 d, p, 3 d, join to 2nd p of last r made, 3 d, join to center p of same r, 3 d, p, 3 d, p, 3 d, close r, turn. Ch, 3 d, p, 3 d, p, 3 d, p, 3 d, turn. R, 3 d, 5 p sep by 3 d, 3 d, close r, turn. Ch, 3 d, join to corresponding p of opposite ch, 3 d, p, 3 d, p, 3 d, turn. R, 3 d, 5 p sep by 3 d, 3 d, close r, turn. Ch, 3 d, p, 3 d, p, 3 d, join to center p of corresponding ch, 3 d, p, 3 d, p, 3 d, join to center p of next ch in 3rd row, 3 d, p, 3 d, p, 3 d, turn and repeat from * all around.

5th Row. * R, 3 d, p, 3 d, join to 2nd p of r in the 3 ring group of 4th row, 3 d, join to center p of same r, 3 d, join to next p of next r of same group, 3 d, p, 3 d, close r, turn. Ch, 3 d, p, 3 d, p, 3 d, turn. R, 3 d, p, 3 d, join to 2nd p of single r in 4th row, 3 d, join to the center p of same r, 3 d, p, 3 d, p, 3 d, close r, turn. Ch, 3 d, 5 p sep by 3 d, 3 d, turn. R, 3 d, p, 3 d, join in 2nd p of last r, 3 d, join to center p of same r, 3 d, p, 3 d, p, 3 d, close r, turn. Ch, 3 d, 5 p sep by 3 d, 3 d, turn. R, 3 d, p, 3 d, join to 2nd p of last r, 3 d, join to center p of same r, 3 d, join to next free p of r in 4th row, 3 d, p, 3 d, close r, turn. Ch, 3 d, p, 3 d, p, 3 d, p, 3 d, turn. Repeat from * all around.

LARGE DOILY

Work same as small doily starting with 92 rings. Attach work to linen at picots of chs.

TATTING INSTRUCTIONS

TATTING ABBREVIATIONS

R . . Ring	L P . Long Picot
L R . Large Ring	Ch . Chain
S R . Small Ring	Sp . Space
D . . Double or Doubles	Sep . Separate
P . . Picot	Cl . Close
S P . Short Picot	

TATTING

Tatting Shuttles are shaped like the *one illustrated*. Some are made with a hook at one end which is used to pull the thread through picots in joining. However, for a beginner the one without a hook is easier to manage as the hook hinders speed and is apt to be in the way. Instead of using the hook to pull the thread through in joining, a crochet hook or a pin may be used. For real dainty tatting use "STAR" Brand Tatting Cotton. It is made in white and a variety of beautiful colors. For heavier tatting use "STAR" Brand Mercerized Crochet Cotton sizes 20 to 50.

WINDING THE SHUTTLE

If the bobbin is removable and has a hole at one side, tie the thread and wind the bobbin until full. If bobbin is not removable wind thread around bobbin in center of shuttle but never allow thread to project beyond the shuttle.

The simplest form of tatting is the ring. This is made with one shuttle only. When making a design of chains and rings two shuttles or 1 ball and 1 shuttle are used.

When a design of rings worked with two colors is made. use 2 shuttles. While learning we suggest using "STAR" Brand Mercerized Crochet Cotton Size 20.

It must be remembered when learning to tat that the knot is made on the shuttle thread and not with it though all action is done with the shuttle thread. This is accomplished by easing the thread around fingers and pulling the shuttle thread taut.

DOUBLE STITCH

Unwind the shuttle so the thread is about 12 inches long. Hold the shuttle between the thumb and forefinger of right hand, with the thread coming from back of bobbin, take the end of thread between the thumb and forefinger of the left hand and pass it around the outstretched fingers, crossing it under the thumb. (Ill. No. 1.)

With the shuttle in your hand, pass the shuttle thread under and over the hand just below the point of fingers. Pass the shuttle between first and second fingers of the left hand, under shuttle and ring thread and bring it back over ring thread allowing the ring thread to fall slack by bringing the four fingers of the left hand together. (Ill. No. 2.) Pull shuttle thread taut and then spread the fingers of left hand till loop is close to fingers and thumb of left hand and pull tight. (Ill. No. 3.) The second half of the stitch is made in the opposite way. Allow the shuttle thread to fall slack, pass shuttle over ring thread and back under ring thread and over shuttle thread. (Ill. No. 4.) Pull shuttle thread taut and tighten ring thread until second half of stitch slips into place beside the first half. (Ill. No. 5.)

By pulling the shuttle thread, the stitch slips back and forth. If it does not, the stitch has been locked by a wrong motion and must be made over again. Practice the doubles until they can be done without looking at instructions. A picot is made by leaving a space between the stitches. (Ill. No. 6.)

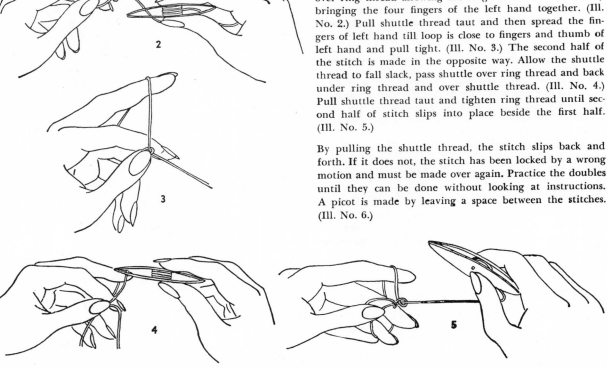

46

RINGS AND PICOTS

Make the first double as directed and work three more double stitches or doubles as they are usually termed.

PICOT. Make the first half of next double, slide it on thread stopping about ¼ inch from last stitch, complete the double and draw entire stitch in position next to doubles made. (Ill. No. 6 and 7.) Work doubles, then work another picot, work doubles, another picot and work doubles. Hold the stitches firmly in the left hand, draw the shuttle thread until the first and last stitches meet forming a ring. (Ill. No. 8.) For larger picots leave a larger space between doubles.

JOINING RINGS

Wind the thread around hand as for first ring and work first double stitch of next ring about ¼ of an inch from ring just made. Work three more doubles.

To join rings. If you are using a shuttle with one pointed end or a hook on one end, insert this end through the last picot of previous ring and pull thread through making a loop large enough to insert shuttle, draw shuttle through the loop and draw shuttle thread tight, this joins the rings and counts as the first half a double. (Ill. No. 9) complete the double, work 3 more doubles then a picot, 4 doubles, picot, 4 doubles, and close ring same as first ring. To reverse work, turn your work so that the base of ring just made is at the top and work next ring as usual.

To join threads. Always join thread at the base of last ring or chain by making a square knot and leaving the ends until work is finished as the strain of working may loosen the knot. Cut ends later. Never attach a new thread in ring as the knots will not pass through the double stitch.

JOSEPHINE PICOTS

Single knots or Josephine picots. This is a series of single knots or just half of a double. Four or five knots for a small Josephine picot and 10 to 12 knots for a larger picot.

WORKING WITH A BALL AND SHUTTLE

All tatting designs containing chains and rings are made with one ball and a shuttle or two shuttles. To make a ring, the thread is wound to circle around the left hand and for the chain thread is wound half way around the hand. Tie the end of ball thread to end of shuttle thread. When you are making a ring use the shuttle thread, when ring is completed turn the ring so the base is held between the thumb and forefinger, place the ball thread over back of fingers winding it twice around little finger to control tension. (Ill. No. 10.) Work the chain over the ball thread using the shuttle thread. When chain is completed draw the stitches close together, drop the ball thread and with shuttle thread work another ring. Picots in chains are made and joined in same manner as in rings.

USING TWO COLORS

When two colors are used in making rings two shuttles must be used. If chains appear on the design with two colors use the second shuttle same as a ball.

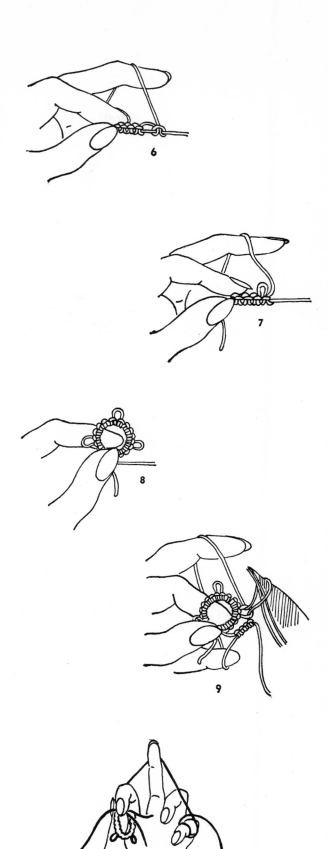